Mack Thomas
The Total Beat

One graduate student's quest for a master's degree and finding more than the author he sought.

Jim Welton

Broken Weather Press
San Antonio, Texas
2016

Copyright © 2016 Jim Welton

All rights reserved.

Published by Broken Weather Press
San Antonio, Texas

Cover Photo of Mack Thomas by Jim Metcalf
Used by permission

ISBN: 0-9978979-0-2
ISBN-13: 978-0-9978979-0-6

DEDICATION

This book would not be possible without the love and support of my family. First my mom, Karen Kramer. I didn't realize it until I started teaching English Language Arts that having a parent who reads is so influential to a child. Mom, thank you for setting the example. To my dad, Ralph Kramer, who I never remember missing a day of work. There were many days when I needed that example. To my late grandparents, Herb and Marie Klaproth, for all the Hardy Boy mysteries they bought for me, they were the best gifts ever. I will carry on the tradition with my grandchildren. To my children, Brian and Lauren, for their dedication to education which inspired me to finish my BA and move on to a MA. To Troy and Charity for earning your own master degrees, your graduations were inspiring. Zach, for your example of hard work and constant enthusiasm.

Finally, to my wife Marvilyn Miller. You bore the brunt of my frustrations, my scheduling needs, my constant need for assurance. You have been with me through the entire process. Your help, advice, and wisdom are throughout all these pages. I am so happy we could share this. Thank you.

Jim Welton

CONTENTS

1	The Search	1
2	On The Road to Santa Fe	11
3	The Interview	35
4	El Rito, New Mexico	51
5	The Road Home	71
6	Postscript	75
7	References	86

ACKNOWLEDGMENTS

I am most grateful to Dr. Rob Johnson. As an undergrad and graduate student I looked forward to every class we shared. You always seemed to be teaching what I was most interested in. Each day in my own classroom I find myself channeling your passion. As I explored thesis topics each idea was born in one of your classes. Dr. David Anshen for your support, efforts, and after class parking lot discussions, I looked forward to those learning opportunities. Dr. Christopher Carmona for your expertise, advice, and social media poetry.

I am also grateful to the nurturers of literature that have crossed my path. The librarian when I was nine years old who decided to waive the two books per checkout rule for the kid who rode his bike in the rain to check out two more books. You made me feel cool for reading.

To Mack Thomas, Irina Thomas, Dr. Jim Metcalf and the others who allowed a stranger into their lives and shared so much. You are in my thoughts each day. I hope I have honored your wishes and this final product was worthy of your time.

Jim Welton

THE SEARCH

I first met Mack Thomas not long after my wife and I experienced a run of luck. I went in search of Mack Thomas partly as a means to my Master's Thesis and partly a fascination with a man who lived countless lives in countless ways. With apologies to Jack Kerouac I call this my year on the road.

My entire knowledge was that Mack wrote two Beat Generation novels back in the 1960s and a second hand comment from my professor Rob Johnson at the University of Texas – Pan American that Mack was gravely ill in the 1970s and quite possibly had not survived to become an octogenarian. Every researcher needs a librarian as a best friend and mine is Gerard Mittelstaedt, a retired library director of the city library in McAllen, Texas. His advice started me down the right path, even though I was destined to teeter along that path, bumping all the way. "It is much harder to prove someone alive than it is to prove they are dead. Go find a death certificate," he said, making it seem as easy as finding my often misplaced sunglasses.

I started with the San Antonio Public Library's web site. I learned that they held a copy of *Gumbo* in their special collections department. I was not certain what qualifies books to be placed in their special collections department or who makes the decision. I still do not. The librarians I spoke with didn't seem to know. Like much of what I discovered about

Mack's life, it just happened to be there. Perhaps Mack was a more significant literary figure than I was thinking. Maybe I had overlooked something and he was much more well-known than I had imagined. After a while I realized when researching the extraordinary you just have to accept things. I had that very morning found an ex-libris copy of *Gumbo* for sale on eBay and had quickly gobbled it up. The sale price of twenty-five cents meant one of the copies, the special collects or the abandoned eBay copy was either overvalued or undervalued. Soon I was on the road, this time to downtown San Antonio and the main branch of the library.

Upon arriving at the main downtown library location I discovered that the seemingly homeless population in San Antonio was very keen on reading and library services. I noticed a small gathering in the parking garage. They were passing a bottle, looking tired, and showing the effects of all night drinking binges. Could this be what a gathering at the Beat Hotel in Paris have looked? Perhaps a meetup in San Francisco after howling at the moon in the Chinese neighborhoods near the wharf? I drew closer to listen to the conversation but my wife guided me away. I needed to focus at the task at hand. That research needed to wait until another day. But I couldn't help wonder if Kerouac would have bought a bottle and shared it with these men and in return had gathered enough stories for a chapter or even a novel.

I quickly navigated the maze of elevators and corridors and located the Special Collection. It was behind the genealogy department, a convenience that would be very fortuitous and later a source of embarrassment. I wandered through the Special Collections, and like every man, refused to ask for directions. I eventually found *Gumbo*, admittedly with a little help. Judging by the dust on the cover, I may have been the first to hold that book in quite a while. The dust jacket held several clues to the author's biography. I looked around to find a copy machine. I should pause here and explain my particular situation.

I was first in college in 1979, I returned to complete a B.A. in 2009, and finally was writing my master's thesis in 2014. My research skills spanned decades. My early skills predated the internet and all of the technology we take for granted today but were updated both by my avocation and vocation. The challenge is knowing when old school or new school would work better. In this case I had clearly chosen the wrong tool for the job. I was greatly surprised to not find a copy machine in the immediate area. I did however see a scanner. As I was struggling with the scanner the librarian took pity on me and asked if I had a cell phone. After confirming I had one of the latest models she asked why I was not just taking pictures like everyone else. Ah, yes of course. This was my first palm to the forehead, there would be many more.

With *Gumbo* in hand I groped for some fact, some hint of who Mack Thomas was. Looking up and seeing the sign Genealogy above me I headed to the desk and hopefully an expert who could help. I explained the research I was doing, specifically to determine if Mack Thomas was dead or alive. I learned that to find the death certificate, in an almost ironic twist, I needed to know where Thomas was born. According to the dust jacket for *Gumbo* "Mack Thomas was born 36 years ago in Texas in what he calls a town of few words almost on the highway between Waco and Hillsboro". This was becoming easier than I thought. The librarian informed me that the library has a subscription to Ancestory.com and that would probably be the best and quickest way to track down any official information on Mack Thomas. "Oh, but he isn't a relative." As I was saying these words I frantically looked for an un-send button. This is my second palm to the forehead moment. I wondered if Boswell had these moments. The words landed with a thud as I turned slightly red. The look on her face was a mix of pity and the unspoken thought how could this person in front of me possibly be a graduate student. "That's ok, you can look up anyone's records," she explained and gently guided me like a newborn to a computer and showed me how to log into library databases and services.

I discovered that there are a lot of people named Mack Thomas in the United States. The dust jacket biography mentioned he was born 36 years ago. The book was first published in 1961. Doing some quick math on a scrap piece of paper I pegged his birth year as 1925. Later I learned it was 1928. There were even quite a few Mack Thomas that were of about the same age. I started to doubt that Mack was his first name at birth. Perhaps it was a nickname he decided upon. Perhaps it was short for Mackenzie. Perhaps his publisher requested a change. I kept widening the net until after an hour of fruitless clicking I gave up for the day. I was going to have to learn where he was born and "somewhere in north Texas near Waco" was not working. Further complicating the search is Waco is in McLennan County and Hillsboro is in Hill County. I returned to my pickup in the parking garage, the earlier gathering had broken up with only an empty bottle in a brown paper sack left behind silently echoing the brotherhood that was shared.

From my home I went in search of a highway map from the late 1920s to see what towns were between those two towns. Again a struggle. The new interstate highway would not have been in existence during that time. I needed a highway map of Texas circa 1925. After days of frustrating searches turned up nothing I learned that prior to the Federal Highway Act in 1956 all maps were local. Now I was back to square one. The history of Interstate 35, which bisects much of Texas from north to south, indicated that at one time Texas Highway 81 followed the same path. That gave me a general path. However further attempts at a smart search were not helping me find Mack Thomas. So it was time to do a dumb search.

I decided to sit at the library logged onto Ancestory.com

until I checked every pencil dot town in Texas if I had to. I learned that it was customary to use the location of the hospital where the baby was born as the place of birth. The first city I selected to try was West, Texas. It was between Waco and Hillsboro and would have been the most likely town to have a hospital. Within minutes I was looking at the birth certificate for Mack Finnis Thomas, Jr. of West, Texas. Born 17 SEP 1928. His father was Mack Finnis Thomas from Alabama and his mother was Leanyaty Chennault from Tennessee. That opened floodgates of information. He appeared in the 1930 census as Mack F. Thomas. By then they were living with his grandfather at "House 412, Dwelling 227, Family 249" in West, Texas. Most important of all, it led to possible addresses. a 1996 address for Mack Thomas 70390 Highway 111 Rancho Mirage, California 92270. There was also another address in Santa Fe, New Mexico which seemed more current.

What I could not find was a working phone number or email address. I would have to use some old school techniques. Kids today may not remember, but way back in the previous century anyone could write an address on an envelope and the US Postal Service would hand deliver it to anyone in the United States. I discovered that service still existed in 2015. After carefully writing, and by writing of course I mean typing, a letter and printing it out, I mailed the letter on February 14th to the Santa Fe address and waited. And waited. And waited. Each day I reacquainted myself with my mailbox, chatted with the postal carrier, and dug eagerly through my mail. I had provided a stamped, self-addressed, envelope that included a plea to return it even if this Mack Thomas was not the man I was searching for. I was looking in the wrong direction.

On March 5th, with the heading Mack Thomas THE author, I received this email.

Dear Mr. Welton

If you are looking for Mack Thomas the author of "Gumbo" and "Total Beast," as well as publicity essays, such as "Death of Edge" and poetry peaces (sic), you have found him. Writing to you is his wife, Irina Thomas. I am aware that there is another author by the name Mack Thomas, but if he is of the Beat Generation as well, the mutation would be hard to connect to the same species. Mack is 86 years old now and bed ridden with all kinds of health problems. Loss of brilliance of mind is not among them...

Your letter was brought to his attention by our secretary, Annie Sahlin. She did write down his response to her questions about Mack's time in Paris. It was as true as Mack is! I am glad that she took the initiative to "stir it" and to make the old volcano spit some sparkles.

If you have any questions to Mack, we will be delighted to try to get answers. Annie will write them down and communicate with you. This e mail address is Mack's address as well.

Please, forgive me for awkward style of writing, I am Russian, twenty-eight years junior to Mack. All the best to you! It will be so interesting to have a glimpse on research you are undertaking.

Sincerely,
Irina Thomas

For the next few moments I may have sounded like the middle school students I taught, "Oh My God! I just heard from Mack Thomas' wife. He's alive, sharp of mind, and they are willing to help" I yelled to my wife from my office upstairs while narrowly missing my keyboard with a stream of coffee I hadn't swallowed. This was to be the start of fascinating extended conversations, which thankfully continues to this day with his wife Irina who is a very talented artist, his lifelong best friend Dr. Jim Metcalf, and best of all, before his passing, with Mack Thomas himself. He has become a bigger than life figure to me who lives a nonfiction version of Forrest Gump's life. He was friends with some of the greatest figures in Beat Literature; William Burroughs, Gregory Corso, Paul Bowles, and Allen Ginsberg. He was also a very talented musician playing with the jazz greats of the day, Thelonious Monk, Miles Davis, Gerry Mulligan, Chip Baker, Gene Harris, and others. Soon after I received Irina's email I heard from Mack's best friend Dr. Jim Metcalf who sent me this in an email:

> I am 70 and met Mack when I was 26 and he was 43 and we have been close friends up until this day. I may have some manuscripts, some poems, and over 40 years of stories about Mack. If you want a man from the Beat Generation....he wrote the jazz column for Alan Ginsberg's "The Evergreen Review" while in prison.
>
> Genius does begin to describe Mack. He has a mind and intellect beyond your wildest expectation. It is almost as if in the last century and a half there is Albert Einstein, Stephen Hawking, and Mack Thomas.
>
> I always described him as a master of all trades and jack of none: author, writer, musician, architect, engineer, master craftsman, poet, philosopher.... His mind will be a gold mine. I am a photographer, among other things. This is Mack on his 86th birthday last Sept. The eyes say it all. (cover photo)
>
> Mack also wrote liner notes for Jazz Albums. Attached is one about Eric Dolphy. He was 37 when he wrote this. Mack can listen to a musician play and give you a rather detailed psychological profile of the musician. I sat and listened to him and a PhD. in music talk about virtually every great composer who ever lived, and Mack not only

knew their music he told him about their psychological profile. After a short visit he will know all about you as well.

You are starting on an adventure that is rarely ever accorded to any writer. To write the story of a genius...When he was in the second grade his teacher gave him an algebra book so he would not be bored. He was a voracious reader of historical novels at five. He knows a lot about everything.

Always be honest and upfront with him, and you will get along well. Remember that Frank Barnes (Mack's character in *The Total Beast*) was willing to die in the shitter, rather than just say I am sorry and to this day, that ain't no bull shit.

When I originally read this it felt like hyperbole for a friend. By the time I finished my journey I realized Metcalf was right.

If I have not grabbed your attention already allow me a brief summary of Mack. Mack was an entrepreneur, successful enough that when I visited him he had two large Mercedes Benz in the garage and a Picasso on the wall. Of course in true Mack Thomas style the Picasso was a gift from Picasso himself. He played golf regularly with "Dandy" Don Meredith and dined with retired presidents. He was an inventor with products ranging from a chromium plated bug deflector to the "Love Mitt" a product he had produced in the small town of El Rito where he owns a private retreat. The Love Mitt was sold through Neiman Marcus and allowed lovers to stroll along holding hands in the coldest weather. He was a screenwriter with a movie deal in place to have George Peppard play him in the adaptation of his second novel *The Total Beast*. He was a professional baseball player barnstorming Texas and Oklahoma, model for Neiman Marcus, Arthur Murray dance instructor, he wrote a jazz column for Evergreen Review, started a diaper service, and much more.

I followed up with a note explaining my mission as a student and the desire for an interview. Shortly thereafter I received a reply from Irina which read in part "Mack read your e-mail and said that he will "not mind" to meet you and talk about writing... which is the most he usually affords anybody and not easily! I think it would be wonderful if you can come to Santa Fe and the sooner is better. Mack was diagnosed with lung cancer last spring and even though he is holding on tough (sic), his strength is seeping away steadily in the last months...". I began thinking, the sooner the better? Spring break starts tomorrow. Would I appear as a lunatic if I asked to visit so quickly? I replied asking to visit that Monday and hoped for the best.

Irina's reply was that 3:00 pm the following Monday would be fine for a visit. That started a frenzy of activity. My wife and I cancelled our plans and set the GPS for Santa Fe, New Mexico and a meeting with Mack Thomas. The next day flew by as I tried to gather information and be prepared for the interview. Early on Sunday morning we were blasting down Highway 10 at eighty miles per hour with the sun rising behind us. It was easy to reflect on all the road scenes in Kerouac's novels while believing we were starting an epic adventure. Two weeks ago I was concerned that I was searching for a death certificate, now I was heading to an interview with Mack. Slowly as the effects of the second large Starbucks coffee took over and the west Texas miles came and went, we began piecing together fragments from a couple emails.

ON THE ROAD TO SANTA FE

I was thankful that Irina had forwarded my information to Dr. Jim Metcalf. Metcalf had begun to coach me about my interview and to fill in some details of Mack's life. One picture began to worry me. It was clear by Irina's statements that Mack was not going to brag about his accomplishments. In fact, getting him to even list his accomplishments may be a problem. She wrote "I know, maybe, just a little more than the dust jackets say about his life... Some people who are still around (his younger brother (84), one old friend who lives in Oklahoma, at least one ex-wife that I know of and numerous lovers) may give you more information, but you have to ask his permission to contact them. And, mind you, do it very cautiously... Or, better yet, take a detour... Mack is very private person and cares not about fame, he NEVER did". If his wife knew little more than the dust jacket version of his life, what chance would I have?

I realized that I was interviewing the real life Frank Barnes of *The Total Beast*. The man who stood up to the toughest guy in the prison and nearly beat him to death. I was rapidly becoming intimidated, both physically and intellectually, by the images Mack's friends were painting. Further, it seemed that if I overstepped my bounds, or made some breech of etiquette, my interview would be scuttled. Suddenly my mind was filled with images of ordering soup from Seinfeld's soup Nazi. Then an e-mail from Metcalf further planted apprehension in my mind. Metcalf wrote:

> I will tell you that Mack has incredible charisma. He could walk into a room and would stand out like Sean Connery. Mack was a guy that no one in Huntsville prison would fuck with face to face, but said that if he went a week without someone trying to kill him, behind his back, it was an unusual occurrence. You may recall in *The Total Beast*, he picked out the baddest ass in the yard and almost killed him, and attacked the brother in the kitchen with a meat cleaver...he always had the look of a man who was incapable of being intimidated by anything or anyone. And a look from him, could make you feel like a small boy...

I began thinking that there are probably better ways to spend spring break in the south. Images of the warm South Padre beaches or the backcountry of Big Bend National Park filled my brain. But I wasn't going to miss this opportunity for anything. By this time the e-mails were ping-ponging back and forth between Irina, Metcalf, and myself. As if I wasn't walking on eggshells already Metcalf offered this advice:

> Insofar, as answering a lot of questions about Mack, I would prefer that you mention to him that I contacted you, offering my input, and if it is ok with him if you talk to me about him. Mack is very much one for protocol. And is a very private man in his own way, and for me to talk more about him, without his permission, is "going behind his back" . . . and might pollute the calm waters you already enjoy.
>
> He won't care. He just wants you to ask. He is very much one for proper manners and protocol. I can advise you to always be upfront with him. He will read you like a

book. If you do anything to violate his system of manners and protocol, or make him feel you went behind his back, even though he would like nothing more in this world than to have you write this paper...you would be gone. Always remember Frank Barnes in the shitter. He would rather die than compromise one small mm of his integrity.

In an e-mail to Irina I had drawn parallels to the Dos Equis "World's Most Interesting Man" advertising campaign. She wrote in reply "What are you missing from the list of all the things Mack did and who he was? You will be surprised, as I still am... prisoner, gigolo, golfer, editor at Evergreen Review in New York, Holy man in Birkenstocks and the bath tub plug on a chain for a necklace on the beach in Carmel ... and never a fraud. Most interesting man never had a chance to be THAT interesting. Yet Mack has never made it any big deal and hardly anybody heard all of his stories. I was hoping to be the somebody to hear all the stories.

While I was being intimidated by the somewhat fictional Mack's alter ego Frank Barnes coming to life I was also concerned about Mack's health. Earlier Irina had written that he was diagnosed with lung cancer. Metcalf had suggested I plan my visit sooner rather than later. Further advice was forthcoming to not tire him out. That we may need to spread the interview over several days. As we stopped for lunch in Fort Stockton, I was still forming an image of who I was meeting. I had been emailed a couple photographs. Metcalf's vocation may have been medicine, but he is also an accomplished photographer who had recently photographed Mack during a visit to Santa Fe. Mack's penetrating blue eyes were evident even in the black and white photo. He definitely looked more like someone who could kick the ass of someone half his age than a tired, frail, patient. I was beginning to feel like the small boy that Metcalf had predicted.

As we pulled back onto the interstate we passed a hitchhiker and I wondered what mad adventure I was missing by not picking him up. But the back seat was loaded with suitcases and snacks and this wasn't the 1950s. Settling into the seat and my thoughts I scanned my iPod for some afternoon tunes. With my thoughts on Mack, Burroughs, and the Beat writers I silently swore to myself for not loading more jazz. All I had was Miles Davis' *Kind of Blue* and that would not last more than 60 miles or so.

The next decision was immediate as we were leaving Ft. Stockton. As it often happens when travelling through the open ranchlands of Texas there were two ways of getting from here to there. A longer but faster route along the interstate or begin the twists and turns of smaller roads north. With my thoughts on Kerouac and *On the Road* I knew that his trips to visit Burroughs in Texas would have taken him on the smaller two lanes through small towns and endless vistas. When Mack was running a diaper service and making deliveries in the area he would have been on these same roads. The choice was made, with Miles Davis providing the tunes we turned north on 285 and made as close to a bee line as we could towards Santa Fe and Mack Thomas.

With my wife as a sounding board and editor, and Miles Davis blowing background music, we began thinking out loud and discussing what we knew about Mack and his life.

Highway 285 begins meandering along a north-westerly route to New Mexico. We began dodging the heavy oil field equipment that was rutting the too narrow dusty road and began discussing Mack Thomas's short story "The Fable of Orby Dobbs" which appeared in a collection of Beat Texas writers that my professor, Rob Johnson, was editing. In the editor's note that accompanied the piece it mentioned that Mack was a young Texan who had met with Burroughs almost daily while they were both living in Paris at the Beat Hotel. At the time my thesis was taking shape as a study of Marxism and Texas Beat writers. I was focusing on Burroughs in Texas so a

Texan like Mack seemed like a perfect addition to my research. Also mentioned in the notes was that he had written "two fine autobiographical novels published by Grove Press in the sixties, *Gumbo* and *The Total Beast*, the latter about his experiences in prison after being arrested on drug charges in Texas." We agreed that even if the interview didn't pan out travelling to Santa Fe to meet Mack and Irina was far more interesting than Burroughs and Marxism. It was also clear that Mack would help shine a light on a period in Texas history when drug users were a bigger threat than communists. This would be in sharp contrast to the relaxing of marijuana laws taking place in America in 2015.

Drug charges in Texas in the fifties and sixties were a nightmare for the person arrested. That was a period of fervent anti-drug campaigning by Texas politicians. For political, and possibly pure social beneficial reasons, Texas politicians were looking down upon drug fiends with a scorn that was usually reserved for communists. A strong anti-drug message led to winning elections, anything perceived as soft on drugs lead to defeat. The message was simple, drug users will do anything to support their habit, steal, assault, murder, anything. Once on drugs any sort of behavior was possible. They will rape your children and destroy America. Once hooked on drugs the only solution was a long prison term, preferably without hope of parole. A small quantity of marijuana that is now sold over the counter could land a person serious prison time. Anything stronger than marijuana and they might throw away the key. Because there were no redeeming values in drug use, there were not many prison novels published in this time, especially in Texas. While Mack did prison time for his crime this was in contrast to Burroughs when he was facing drug charges in Louisiana. When his lawyer said things were not looking good for an easy acquittal, Burroughs left the Texas border where he had been a farmer growing onions and citrus and headed to Mexico to allow the statute of limitations to run out before returning.

Also in the notes was a reference that Mack had met Burroughs in the late 1950s in Paris. Now for most readers the assumption would be Paris, France and in this case that would be correct. However, Texans may be thinking of the other Paris. The small city in east Texas located about halfway between Dallas and the Arkansas border and a couple hundred miles up the road from Burroughs's old farm in New Waverly. So in a small bit of irony they were in Paris, France discussing east Texas that would have included the area around Paris, Texas.

Placing Mack in Paris during the "Beat Hotel" era was exciting. His daily visits with Burroughs would have brought him in touch with many of that era's most influential Beat Generation writers and artists. Two more items appeared in the as of yet unpublished manuscript that Rob Johnson was editing. "He and Burroughs read together in the Bowery in April of 1964 at a party hosted by artist Wynn Chamberlain." This meant their relationship carried on past the Paris days and for several years later including after Mack was released from prison. Mack appeared to be showing up at the right places with the right people. Yet he was not well known to the general public. Finally, Ted Morgan, Burroughs's biographer, interviewed Mack for his book *Literary Outlaw the Life and Times of William S. Burroughs*. A reading list had taken shape.

Both of Mack's books were out of print but as noted earlier, easy to find on eBay. Ted Morgan's biography of Burroughs was recently updated in 2012 and a new copy was ordered and delivered in a couple days. This had allowed me time for a quick read of Mack's books and a chance to read what Morgan had used in his biography on Burroughs. I didn't want to be thumbing through the books when interviewing Mack, so we began highlighting selected passages beginning with Literary Outlaw.

Morgan introduces Mack Thomas as a "saxophone-playing

young Texan" who "was one of the young men who liked to drop in on Burroughs and talk." It wasn't until later in the paragraph that Morgan mentions that Mack would "go on to write two autobiographical books that displayed considerable talent". We'll discuss the two books later, but of note here is the quote "displayed considerable talent." In less than a day I would be asking Mack why he wrote only two books. Why, when I was researching, did I not find more information on the books? The list of questions was building.

There was a confirmation of an earlier comment that Jim Metcalf had made. Morgan writes that Mack "was perceptive in his appraisal of Burroughs." Metcalf had written almost the same thing about his friend. He mentioned that Mack was very skilled in sizing people up quickly, that he could figure out someone quickly after meeting them. Further adding to my building anxiety was thinking about what perception Mack would have of me. Morgan valued Mack's perception enough to devote a few more paragraphs to what Mack thought of Burroughs.

Later in *Literary Outlaw* Morgan discusses the legal struggles that Burroughs was once again in over drugs. As the trial was working its way through the French legal system Burroughs "compared himself to his young friend Mack Thomas. who had recently been sentenced in Texas to twenty years for heroin possession". I was unable to clear up this contradiction. Morgan is claiming heroin possession, everyone else I interviewed claimed it was marijuana. This is evidence that Thomas and Burroughs had stayed in touch after Thomas had left Paris. Morgan also offers a glimpse into what Thomas would have experienced. Thomas had told Burroughs that he (Thomas) "had been busted at the height of an antinarcotic crusade under Governor Price Daniels. The feeling in Texas, where Burroughs had once grown marijuana, was rabid - dope fiends were worse than murders." Morgan continues, "Thomas had gone through a nightmare, upon which he wrote his 1965 book, *The Total Beast*." Morgan was not exaggerating about the nightmare." When the police questioned him, they handcuffed him around a tree and hooked up electrodes to his balls and to the alternator of their car -- if you weren't talkative, that made you think twice." And once in prison, things would not be any easier. "In prison if you died in the summer, your autopsy would read 'sunstroke', and if you died in the winter, it would say 'pneumonia'. Burroughs knew he was a lucky man to be out of Texas and out of the United States at that time." While Burroughs was lucky, I was flying up Highway 285 almost to New Mexico to interview the man who was unlucky. I was also thinking about the technique that Thomas had taught Burroughs to get rid of unwelcome visitors.

Burroughs was being constantly interrupted by fans and the curious knocking on his door at the Beat Hotel. Burroughs explained to friends that he was working on a technique that was "shown to him by Mack Thomas, for getting rid of unwanted callers. Being polite, he would invite them in, and then he would stare at them while repeating to himself, 'I love you, I hate you, I love you, I hate you," and usually they became so uncomfortable, they left. If that didn't work, he would visualize their spirit outside the door, and if the picture was strong enough the body would soon follow". So far the image I was forming of Thomas was intimidating at the least and damn right frightening at the worst. Did Thomas extend this polite invitation expecting me to never show up? Was he talked into it? That passage would occasionally return to my thoughts as I interviewed Thomas.

Mack Thomas once again appears in Morgan's biography of Burroughs, this time in New York in the early summer of 1965. What is of interest here are the who's who of New York society that were at an event with Burroughs and Thomas. Obviously Burroughs is the draw, but as we will see throughout Thomas' life, Thomas is surrounded by gifted, talented people. The event was a reading in the loft of Wynn Chamberlain. On page 437 Morgan describes the scene:

Mack Thomas The Total Beat

In the vapor-lamp dusk, a line of derelicts waited for admittance to the Bowery Mission, while across the street, at 222 Bowery, a former Y.M.C.A. the glitterati assembled to meet a man whose reputation had been enhanced by his absence from the New York scene. The sculptress Marisol was there, with a green bow tie in her hair, and the poets Ron Padgett and Ted Berrigan and Frank O'Hara, and the photographers Diane Arbus and Richard Avedon, and the painters Larry Rivers and Larry Poons and Barnett Newman and Andy Warhol.

It has been 50 years since this event and some of the names may not be familiar to most readers. A couple of examples of projects from the guests would include Marisol who would go on to create a sculpture of Hugh Hefner which graced the cover of *Time Magazine* and eventually found its way to the Smithsonian Institute. The sculpture is perhaps best known as showing Hefner with two of his trademark pipes. Ron Padgett as a high school student started a literary magazine and fearlessly solicited works by some of the best writers of the day. Amazingly Jack Kerouac, Allen Ginsberg, and other notable writers submitted articles to the new venture *The White Dove*. He later followed in their footsteps and attended Columbia University. Diane Arbus is recognized by critics as one of the leading female photographers of her time. She specialized in portraits of people that were on the fringes of society or those that would be described as ugly by many people. Of the artists, Barnett Newman is recognized as a leader in abstract expressionism. In 2014 one of his paintings, Black Fire, sold for over $84,000,000. And of course, Andy Warhol needs no introduction. With this collection of talent in the room is it any wonder that the event was described as a "quorum of the downtown art scene, a charged, electric, high energy event, recognized as such by *The New York Times*, who sent a reporter to cover it. Mack Thomas, Burroughs friend from the Beat Hotel days, and recently sprung from a Texas jail, read from his boyhood memoir *Gumbo* and sang Methodist hymns with his East Texas drawl".

Gumbo. My copy had once been in circulation at the Nampa Carnegie Library in Nampa, Idaho. A faded pencil note records these facts. "3/65 McN. 3.50." Across the bottom appears an ugly red stamp which had come crashing down hard on the book with the word WITHDRAWN at an angle. There were no signs of wear, each page crisp and free of dog ears. The dust jacket was pristine. I hoped to find a random note, a passage underlined to affirm that someone circulated the novel. With the singular exception to some yellowing of the pages the book was the same as it first appeared on that library shelf fifty years earlier. Had anyone in Nampa, Idaho taken that novel home? It didn't seem so. And would Nampa, Idaho actually be a town where a Beat *novel* would be popular? A quick Wikipedia search revealed Nampa is close to Boise, and that it's most famous resident was Pete Lindsey, the front man for the rock and roll band Paul Revere and the Raiders. Why would a librarian in Idaho, arguably the most un-Beat state in the union, spend $3.50 of their budget on this Beat novel? The answer is on the copyright page.

"Several sections from this novel were previously published: "Magnolia", "Folksong", and "Revival" in *Evergreen Review*; "Fig Newton", "Hard-Rock Candy", and "Apple" in *Saturday Evening Post*; "Green Grapes" in *Cosmopolitan*" (*Gumbo*). *Saturday Evening Post* and the 1960s version of *Cosmopolitan*. Could anyone imagine a chapter from a Burroughs novel, perhaps *Queer*, appearing in those magazines? The editorial comments that appear on the dust jacket, of course written carefully to sell books, highlights why magazines who targeted women readers would find this material perfect to publish.

After the perfunctory platitudes of this being a "moving book", by an "authentic new talent in American writing", and offering evidence such as "leading magazines have already recognized Mack Thomas' remarkable achievement" the dust jacket review begins to set the stage for what readers could expect from this "source of wonder and delight." This is a "warm, tender story of a boy in Texas during the thirties (and) has as its scope the rich, magical world of childhood". What will make this novel unique is "a picture of poverty suffused with a glow of nostalgia for the warm and happy days of childhood. It is the picture of the depression viewed by a new generation".

Closing the book and looking at the back cover there is a picture of Mack Thomas. Like most of the black and white photographs made in the 1960s this makes Thomas look older than his 36 years. Leroy McLucas, the photographer who made a career out of photographing jazz players and writers for covers and book sleeves, along with his more artistic works, posed Thomas with the sleeves on his checked shirt casually rolled up, a book or maybe a manuscript trying to look random on the table. What is invisible in the photo are Thomas' piercing blue eyes. His friend Jim Metcalf described the younger Mack as "Hollywood handsome" and this photograph would certainly back that claim. It is easy to see him modeling suits for Neiman Marcus or taking center stage and blowing an extended jazz improvisational piece while ladies swooned and men took notice.

The cover photograph, with a yellow or sepia tone, features a small young boy of perhaps five or six looking vulnerable. His gaze is facing down and to the right of the camera. His shirt appears simultaneously too big around the chest and too short in the sleeves. His small hand is covering his mouth; he may be sucking his thumb or perhaps biting his nail. The light hints at a setting sun, or maybe a rising sun. The photo dominates the cover taking up a full 90% of the available space. On the bottom, unceremoniously, reads *Gumbo* a Novel by Mack Thomas. *Gumbo*, in black, almost blends in with the dark background of the picture resting above it. Mack Thomas, in green, pops out. This is common when the author is bigger than the book, think James Patterson or Nicholas Sparks, but this is a debut author. The publisher, Grove Press, was banking on readers having read the excerpts in their favorite magazine.

Taking *Gumbo* in my hands I realized I would soon be reading a novel that was autobiographical in nature. I turned to the first page and was introduced to Mack Thomas appearing as a young boy named Toby. "When the sky got dark and clapped its hands, Toby wrapped himself in a blanket and sat on the wooden porch that mouthed the front of the house, watching the noisy sky make blue-white cracks that healed at once without a trace of a scar." The opening chapter, "Magnolia", like most opening chapters introduces us to the characters and the setting. The weather storm that was brewing as Toby sat and watched transitioned to the economic storm that was gripping the world. The economic storm revolved around work and like most families during the depression work would fill their minds and be key to their survival.

"By the time the leaves got too dirty to keep and the trees started throwing them away, Toby knew that 'work' was something that Papa got at the mill. The mill was the biggest house in the world. It was white and had four rows of windows. Everyone got 'work' at the mill, all of the Papas and most of the Mommas, to". Thomas is filling his opening chapter with dark, dirty, and cold images. It is easy to see where this is leading, but Thomas does so in a gentle way. While describing a time when Toby was terrified from seeing an airplane for the first time, Thomas perfectly creates a tension that builds then at the last moment turns and gently lands.

Thomas writes in *Gumbo* "One day, waiting for Papa to beat the dark to the house, Toby saw a thing in the sky, coming across the top of the mill" the thing "made a noise like a busy bee caught in each ear. It came slow through the almost star time sky and looked like a Toby eater. He got too scared to notice he had pulled an arm off Celia's pickaninny doll." As the "Toby eater" was disappearing he heard someone crying.

"Listening made it Celia's. He ran to her without another thought about the thing that hunted in the sky. Rounding the corner, he saw her standing by the back steps, holding the doll and the loose arm to herself and trying to stop crying." All the commotion brought Mamma out of the house where she "looked at Celia and doll and arm and Toby" then "stepped back in the kitchen for a few seconds, then came out and down the three steps, the stinging stick in her hand".

Before the stinging stick could be wielded and the punishment administered, Celia hides Toby in her dress and explains that Toby didn't mean it and should not be punished. Momma then "took Celia by the hand and reached into Celia's skirt and found Toby. He knew by the way her arm felt on his elbow that it was all right to come out. She aimed all of their eyes with her own, aimed them at the mill. After a bit she said, 'We'd better get on in the house. It's getting dark'". Thomas is masterful in handling this extended metaphor. The "Toby eater" flying directly over the mill which showed Toby's lack of sophistication and worldly knowledge. Toby's innocence was reinforced by Celia who kept him from being punished for something he had not intended to do. Thomas expertly portrays Momma's, mercy and wisdom along with capturing the tender moment when she touched his elbow. The final touch, everyone looking at the mill as darkness descends could easily have been a hackneyed and cliché riddled passage. Instead the scene settles into a gentle rhythm as they return to the safety and security of the house. Immediately Thomas drops the bomb that readers would have been waiting for.

"Not long after the cold came, Papa stopped leaving every morning. There seemed to be lots of Papas around, and the mill noise had died. Papa didn't smell like work anymore." Bad things happen to good people. The depression had come to Toby's world. Mack avoids telling the audience it was a sad and dark time where life seems to have been sucked out of the world, instead Mack paints this picture explaining that Papa "walked to the mill every day and stood by the little white house at the mill gate, talking with the other Papas and looking into the naked branches of the cottonwood trees. He took Toby with him now and then. The Papas stood around making marks on the ground with their blunt toes of their shoes, talking in low voices, not laughing too often or for very long when they did. Gathering the crisp brown leaves into playing piles, Toby looked up from time to time and found Papa watching him with a hurt in his eyes." The desperation of a father trying to provide for his family glides off the paper. Even though this chapter first appeared in the Evergreen Review, it is easy to see how readers of Cosmopolitan or the Saturday Evening Post would have enjoyed the story.

Eventually the family was split apart briefly as Papa headed to Mississippi for work. Help from the community was described as "The man who brought the flat little sack with a picture and wigglies came with another one a few days later. This one had something that Mamma called 'money'. Again, note the innocence that Thomas gives to the character Toby. Toby is growing up blissfully unaware of the family's plight which was about to get better.

Thomas continues to use weather and nature metaphors, this time to bring good news. "One-day Toby went outside to the toilet and ran back in the house with a shout. 'The sun's gettin' mad again, mad again, mad again!'. It wasn't long before the trees started speckling themselves with new leaves". Bright, warm sunshine and new life on the trees could only mean one thing. "Orby's Papa came to see Mamma. 'Write Tobias,' he said. 'The mill is startin' up again next week". The subsequent reunion is written with the same easy going style and warmth that was unexpected from the buildup I had. This chapter lives up to the dust jacket hype of being warm and tender.

"Green Grapes" first appeared in *Cosmopolitan* magazine in the early 1960s. During this time *Cosmopolitan* magazine was a general interest publication. This was in the years before editor Helen Gurley Brown would transform it into the format and content that modern readers are familiar with. Articles on the birth control pill or "Five Ways to Drive Him Crazy" and "Have the Best Sex Ever Tonight" were a few years off. Still influencing the editorial staff were the days that Cosmopolitan was a literary magazine looking for great writers. Readers were treated to this story about Toby and the school teaching principal who lived next store.

Toby had just woken up from a nap on a pallet located on the front porch when "he heard a good sound. . . a sound like the kind Mr. Cuna'ham made when he was doing something at his worktable under the big tree in his back yard next door". The next couple pages are a treat as Thomas spins in vivid detail the route that Toby takes to reach the source of the sound. "Bare foot on warm dirt whirled him from the naked fence and shuttled him under the leaves". The barefoot being a reminder of the economic times and the carefree days of childhood. Another example of the mastery Thomas has over nature images is displayed as he writes "wire, crosses of hickory posts and summers and winters and springs had made each row in the tiny vineyard a tunnel of leaves. The tunnels were veins where magic flowed its secret and wonderful things. The leaves caught the sunlight and shifted its scorch to a praying-mantis green that the eager green grapes would learn to love in a ripening week or two". Toby was exploring a magical world and the reader is carried away with him.

Toby eventually remembers why he had come this way and finds "Mr. Cuna'ham, a short round man with hair as black as his eyes, standing solid at the end of a solid wooden worktable, cranking a handle that turned a wheel that made blades of hoes and knives sharp again". According to Papa "Mr. Cuna'ham had more sense than the rest of the teachers all put together." Thomas goes on to say that "Mr. Cuna'ham could take his yard mower apart and put it back together again and it would work. He could fix clocks and make whistles out of acorns and build birdhouses and make rubber guns and carve propellers that turned in the wind and one time made a shoe box fly like a kite. But the best thing is he liked to tell things, like what made the kite stay up in the first place". Later I would discover that Thomas could do all these things and more. He also had the kind of genius that demanded to know why. Psychologists and other scientists will debate the nature versus nurture issue, but as this book is autobiographical it appears that Thomas was fortunate to grow up next to someone that could nurture his natural talent. In the next paragraph Thomas as Toby also displays the ability to size people up which was mentioned by Metcalf and Irina Thomas.

"Toby saw that it would be a good day for talking. Mr. Cuna'ham shirt was wet and when that happened he liked to put his hand inside his shirt and scratch. There was no way of knowing how it worked but the talking was better when there was scratching". Toby was still hiding in the vineyard, eating grapes, and hoping Mr. Cuna'ham would see him. Toby would shake the vines in an attempt to get Mr. Cuna'ham's attention. With that not working Toby decided to just come out into the open. Has he began enacting his plan "a bunch of green grapes happened to be in a good place and Toby backed through the leaves and leaned on the vines to reach them." Toby was caught. Mr. Cunningham called over to Toby "You're caught red handed so come on out of there . . . that's it, come on over here. Well you ought to look guilty, I don't blame you, tearing my vines and stealing, didn't I tell you what to expect if you eat green grapes!" While trying to decide what to do with Toby, Mr. Cunningham had Toby pull up a nail keg to use as a chair.

After Toby was seated on the nail keg Mr. Cunningham makes certain Toby wasn't going to run off and heads into the house. Once again Toby is seemingly in trouble. Mr. Cunningham returned with "his serious look and to the table under the tree and started setting the pair of jelly glasses and the pitcher of lemonade on the weathered boards. Filling the glasses and untying the napkins to get at the oatmeal cookies, he made his voice rough as he said, Now Toby, you'll have to eat three or four cookies and drink enough of this lemonade to make them pack down around all those green grapes about to make trouble in your stomach." Once again a wise adult has withheld punishment and shows mercy towards Toby. This time, with a lesson on life.

Mr. Cunningham went on to talk about three baby birds that he and Toby had watched and how Toby would never want to hurt a growing thing. Mr. Cunningham appears to be struggling with his thoughts. "You see, Toby, he stalled, searching for words, "growing thing . . . living things, are making a trip . . . going somewhere, on their way from what they are to what they can be". After watching an adult bird fly easily from a fence post to a peach tree Cunningham continued. "See how easy it made it to the peach tree? Well those baby birds, that's where they're going . . . getting big and pretty and able to fly like that. We'll look out before long and see those baby birds all grown up and perching on fence posts unless something stops them. We've got to help growing things if we can, you and me, help them to get where they are going and not do anything that might stop them or make it harder than it has to be." Then Thomas brings the story, and the lesson full circle to the grapes. "Like those green grapes out there, trying to get big and soft and full of good juice instead of staying little and hard and green like they are now." Finally, the real lesson emerges. "I want you to know it's kittens and peaches, and every growing thing in the world. People it's about people, most of all."

Toby quickly connects the lesson with his life and asks if it's about his younger brother Pud. Assured that it is about Pud , a mystery that had been puzzling Toby suddenly becomes clear and he asks Cunningham "'Is that what brother means?'

Well wait a minute, now! Mr. Cunningham scratching hard. 'Yes by golly! That's what it means'". With this new knowledge Toby runs home to share the lesson with his brother.

The best example of Thomas' ability to write interestingly in great detail occurs in the chapter named "Apple" which first appeared in the *Saturday Evening Post*. Thomas takes five pages to carefully tell the story of Papa peeling an apple for the family. Of course so much more was taking place than just the peel coming off and the solitary apple being divided among the children. The story begins with the family gathering around Papa as he prepared the apple. Thomas writes "Papa pinched the apple stem between two left fingers and held it so it wouldn't turn without his right hand on the apple. Celia, Jenny, and Toby counted the turns in their heads with the ABC's, knowing that the letter that broke the apple stem would be a clue for the name of the one they would marry. Pud didn't know such secret magic and counted the turns with blinks of his rounding eyes." This appears to be a regular family scene with rituals and rules. Remember the story takes place during the depression. An apple would be a treat and a diversion for the family. A couple paragraphs later Papa is still peeling the apple. Thomas writes:

> Papa stripped the apple with care, feeling a kind of duty to keeping the peel in a single piece. More than that, it seemed somehow to have something to do with not being disappointed with himself, setting a good example. The knife was another of his fingers and ribboned the skin as if unspooling a secret. Halfway down the apple's cheek a shallow brown scar made him frown. He paused to tidy the scar, and Pud scooted nearer the floor. The edge Toby felt over Pud because of the almost two years he had on him wasn't enough to let him keep sitting still with Pud that close to Papa. Something he did in his muscles and bones made his chair seem to pour him on the floor and slide him silently across the living room linoleum, over its fat roses and lacy green leaves to a spot that would make the

edge of age enough again.

Thomas continues the silent tension. "By now Papa had it almost naked. The ribbon was down to the trickiest part. To do it right from now on he had to turn the apple upside-down, but that meant running the risk of tangling and maybe breaking the ribbon". Not since William Carlos Williams observed a red wheelbarrow has a common everyday item caused such concentration and meaning. Continuing:

> Papa explained the predicament he was in. "Do we break it off now and peel out the bottom separate, or take a chance on trying to get it all?"
>
> "Turn it," Pud urged.
>
> "Get it all in one piece!" said Toby.
>
> Jenny copied Celia and Mamma and didn't butt in, knowing some way that this was man's work.
>
> "That's about the way I feel about it," answered Papa. He did all the things he needed to do, being careful with the peel, and after an anxious minute he held up the knife with the peel turned down from the tip in one long apple spring." After first offering it to Jenny who "made a face like eating green persimmons" the peel was evenly divided between Pud and Toby. As Papa began the task of dividing the apple between the kids, Celia declined her piece explaining "'you know how there's times when you crave a thing and times when you don't, Papa,' she answered quietly." Clearly Celia at 16 was growing up and becoming an adult. This caused Toby to think about the same thing. As he laid in bed he was "grinning in the dark and grinned his mind all the way to wondering how it would feel to give Pud his part of the apple. A thought and a doze and a wondering later he wondered how it would be to have a whole apple all to himself. Something about it wouldn't let him wonder about it for long, and sailed his mind to a

glass jar of light at the core of a whole, dark, pungent apple of sleep."

Mack skillfully manages to create a nostalgic mood for sharing not just an apple, but the ceremony and family that surrounded it.

There are many more stories and lesson learned in *Gumbo*, both easy and difficult. After all, this was the depression in the rural south. Returning to the present, we were leaving a dusty corner of Texas and began seeing signs for Carlsbad Caverns in New Mexico. We stopped for a cold drink, a bathroom, and a chance to stretch. With all the modern oil field traffic barreling down the highway, and newly opened franchises lining the road hoping for their chance at the lotto like profits that fracking brought to oil country, it was hard to imagine the Texas that Mack had grown up in. I had so many questions to ask about his teachers, school, and family, and growing up. But first there were the adult chapters of his life to think about. The chapters in his life covered by *The Total Beast* and his time in prison.

It doesn't take long for Thomas to establish that *The Total Beast* tells the story of a very different person than Toby in *Gumbo*. If a reader happened to read the two books back to back and not separated by the three years between publications, it is easy to immediately feel empathy for the sweet kid who marveled at his dad's ability to peel an apple. The first location in *The Total Beast* is far away from his idyllic boyhood home. Thomas opens *The Total Beast* with these lines:

He knew there was a building. The building was easy to imagine with its deliberate mass and tombstone seriousness standing ten floors tall on a city block at the end of the world on Main Street. He knew the building was divided into courts and customized cubes for judges, clerks, hunters, keepers, and criminals and that some of the cubes were made of marble and oak and others of thick metal plate and tempered steel bars. He knew there was a barred cell in a remote wing of the top floor County Jail, a special cell with a solid steel door in the rear wall. He knew there was a small windowless room behind that solid door, and that it held on its concrete floor a concrete box four feet wide, four feet long, and four feet high, with walls six inches thick. He knew why the prisoners of the County Jail called it 'the Shitter'.

I was remembering that multiple sources, including his wife and best friend, have said this is an autobiographical novel. I also knew from my background reading that he spent time in prison in Texas. It seems that his first stop was in a county jail. It was hard for me not to forget Jim Metcalf's comment that Frank Barnes (Thomas) would rather have died in the Shitter than sacrifice his principles. When I first read Metcalf's comments I really didn't connect with the details of the Shitter. Now I was connecting the 4x4x4 concrete tomb, the 43 days Thomas spent inside, and the man I was driving to meet.

Thomas at some point portrays himself as a sweet child in *Gumbo*, then a tough, mean, son of a bitch in *The Total Beast*. In between was the sax playing, model, dance instructing, Hollywood handsome charmer. A sociologist in the 1950s may have blamed it on Mack's drug use while agreeing that long term prison time was the only solution. This certainly would have fit with the attitude in Texas. As noted earlier, Burroughs would be receiving much different treatment in France a year or so later.

The beauty in which Mack described the apple peeling is in sharp contrast to the first dining scene in *The Total Beast*. Barnes had been in the Shitter for 43 days and had eaten only bread and water during that time. After being transferred from the county jail to a new facility, Barnes was processed and eventually found himself in the chow line. "The mess hall mulligan came to the serving line and ladled and forked a sticky paste of navy beans, dry boiled carrots, thin brown gravy, a boiled potato and a slice of fried baloney from the inserts in the steam table. At the end of the serving line a deep tin held day-old bread. He took four slices and moved on." Later, after being shown to his new cell and meeting Charlie his cell mate, there was "trouble between his stomach and the food. A bitter flood poured down his tongue too fast to swallow and he rode the spasm to his feet. he turned and dropped his hands to the rim of the toilet bowl. Charlie sat up on the bunk and watched. When his stomach was empty he pushed up and leaned against the wall spitting thick strings down into the bowl."

Mack would deal with all sorts of unpleasant to horrific memories. While not happening directly to Frank Barnes, Mack's character, from *The Total Beast* it was a glimpse into the horrible events that took place in the prison. One evening Mack and his cell mate Charlie were awake and heard a voice that

"had been coaxing was now loud and threatening. "'I said roll over!'

Charlie chuckled and got up grinning. 'Listen to that shit! That's old Sunshine, in the cell on top of us. I told him yesterday that kid wasn't no punk!'

Charlie moved against the bars and stood listening to the struggle in the cell above. A scream began but was choked back into the lungs that tried to build it, then there was a noise like someone crying with a strong hand cupped across his mouth.

Charlie dropped his hands from the bars and scratched his belly. 'Well it sounds like Sunshine made a punk out of him now!'"

Deftly writing about an experience that is the source of jokes to people who have never experienced prison, but a nightmare for those who had, Mack displays his considerable writing talents. Later revenge is administrated by the cellmate and delivered in a style reminiscent of Ernest Hemingway. Thomas writes:

A chest blow rammed through the snores of Quarantine. One of the snores ended with a grunt of painful surprise.
A second voice screamed with a grief raging beyond consolation. "You fucked me!"
A second blow fell and a gasp extended in a voice that began in agony and soared into terror. "Wait . . . wait!"
"What the fuck"
"Hey!"
"All right knock that shit off!"
"You fucked me!"
"Oh God no no wait!"
He (Barnes) dropped his legs over the side and sat up.
Charlie whirled and shook him by the knees "It's Sunshine!"
"You fucked me!"
"Help!"
"What the fuck is going on?"
"I said knock that shit off!"
"Somebody is getting his ass wiped, Boss!"
"You stupid bastard!"
"You fucked me!"
"No no please . . ."
Charlie rushed to the front of the cell, climbed on the toilet and put his head against the arch at the top of the bars.
"You fucked me, you fucked me!"
"Oh God you've already killed me . . ."
"You fucked me!"

A loud gurgling scream faded to a brief wet rattle and the pleading voice stopped.

This is a long way from the subject matter of *Gumbo*. It also highlights the range of writing talent that Mack possessed. He could make your parental heart reach out to hold a small schoolboy in *Gumbo* then turn around in *The Total Beast* and cause heartbeats to race as he describes the murder of a rapist. Knowing this was autobiographical made the tension seem even worse.

Rumble strips from the shoulder of the road startled me into the present. Thoughts of Mack in prison were pushed aside as I tried to remember the 100 miles of Texas highway we had just travelled. I looked around, had it been 100 miles? Nothing seemed to have changed. It was the same oil field traffic, the same tired farmland yearning to be free. The music had stopped and I needed time to plan the interview.

THE INTERVIEW

As we headed north and the signs of New Mexico became more frequent, we discussed the interview. My career began in sales and marketing where I rose to the position of Vice President of a large multi-national corporation. An interview of a writer who invited me into his home should be simple because there were no profits or jobs hinging on the outcome of this meeting as often were in my previous career. So why was I so nervous? His friends seemed surprised that Mack was offering the interview. He had nearly beaten a man to death while in prison. He did write one of the most touching and sentimental novels I have ever read. It was easy to see how this interview could go in any direction.

"What are you going to wear?" I was a bit startled when I heard my wife ask the question.

"I don't know, I forgot what I brought. I guess a nicer shirt and slacks, business casual."

"What should I wear?"

"I don't know, what did you bring . . .?"

Focusing on such a simple subject took some of the edge off. I finally decided that business casual would offer a proper sign of respect. With that important decision made, I could again focus on driving and reaching Santa Fe. We arrived in Santa Fe and quickly found our hastily chosen hotel. It's spring break and Santa Fe seems to have an influx of tourists. We had called several hotels before finding space here. The location was close to downtown with easy access to the main roads that would take us south to Mack's address. After lugging the luggage up a flight of stairs, I realized I may have discovered the root of the word luggage. After a great dinner and drinks we planned our itinerary for the next day. Our appointment with Mack was at 3:00 pm leaving us time to visit some of our favorite sights in Santa Fe, enjoy a couple of meals and drive up into the hills near the new community college that Mack calls home.

Of course I had earlier used Google Street View to locate the house and take a look. On my computer screen his home looked to be part of a master planned community of cookie cutter modest adobe style homes. It may have been a retirement village like many that fill vacant land in the south for retirees from the north. The front yards were small and generally without grass. As we drove through the neighborhoods I realized that my earlier assumption was wrong. The homes were about twice the size as I had imagined. It did seem that all the brick was made the same way at the same factory, but there were differences in the homes. Where cars were visible, they were late model luxury models. I could easily spot the nannies and maids busily working. The past few decades must have been good to Mack. I felt my pulse quicken a bit as we found his street, then his house. As I parked, my truck seemed out of place in the neighborhood. I gathered my tools - a notebook, recorder, pens, and strode towards the door with my wife who was starting to feel like my shield against the world.

I'm not certain what I expected as I rang the doorbell but I know it was not Irina. Dressed casually in a white silk blouse and black slacks she simultaneously evoked a casual charm and formal presence. She had mentioned in an email that she is an artist and a quick scan around the home made that clear. If these were her works of art she should have added that she was a highly talented artist. Without a chance to gather my bearings with all the artwork, my attention was drawn back to Irina. Every politician would love to have her genuine friendly smile and welcome. My wife and I immediately liked her. Irina is very warm and welcoming with a quiet confidence. She is also a several decades younger than Mack. After inviting us into the living room she announced to Mack that we had arrived.

As their housekeeper put the finishing touches on the kitchen we sat down and began looking around the house. It was much larger than Google Street View let on. Works of art, in various stages of completion were everywhere. The formal dining room, living room, and art nook were in the front of the house along with two guest bedrooms. The kitchen and casual family room is in the middle of the house with a bright courtyard just off the breakfast nook. A hallway led to what we presumed was the garage and back door. Finally, the owner suite where Mack was resting was just around the corner. It was easy to see where Mack held court. A comfortable chair was across from the couch were we sat. Books and papers were on the side table next to the chair. As I gathered my thoughts Mack entered the room and said hello. He was dressed casually in a white tee shirt and light blue pajama bottoms. Metaphorically and physically he seemed larger than life even with his illness.

His eyes are what people notice first. Even in a room of blue eyed people, Mack's eyes would stand out. Searing, intense, lively and bored at the same time. His eyes were in contrast to the tired nature of his shuffling gait. He had been in bed and was dealing with the usual effects of getting out of bed combined with the health issues he was battling. Slightly stooped over and a little short of breath, he sat down. I could feel him studying me, then Marvilyn. I forget what he said first, I was realizing what a physically powerful man he must have been. It was easy to picture him commanding a stage, saxophone in hand, on a wild improvisational rift. Or the ladies swooning as he took their hand to teach them the latest dance at Arthur Murray's. I was picturing a much younger Mack on a pitcher's mound in baseball which is raised about 10 inches from the level of the batter. Intimidation was probably one of Mack's greatest advantages when he was playing baseball. It was certainly working on me in this situation.

I should mention right here that Mack's health is not the best. While the rumors of his passing were greatly exaggerated, he is over 80. During our conversations his memory would fail him at times. Medication has added pounds to his athletic frame, gravity is pulling him back to earth. At times Irina or a friend would make suggestions and help him remember, sometimes it helped, other times he would say "I guess" or "if you say so." For other men it would be tempting to think he would use it as an excuse to not answer a question. I never sensed that. Mack is a no nonsense, give it to you straight, kind of man who I doubt ever hid from anything. What he remembered, he remembered with confidence and clarity. He also never calculated his answers and how they would make him appear.

I had hoped to ask a couple questions and have Mack start telling stories. That would have been too easy. That is for people who are trying to be famous or care what others think about them. That is not Mack. I would ask a question, receive a direct answer, then silence. Occasionally I would shuffle a paper, write down some notes, and allow silence to fill the space, hoping Mack would jump in. He rarely did. Instead he watched. And as he watched I was increasingly reminded of my own shortcomings. I thought I had prepared enough questions to fill days, they were lasting minutes. My usual quick wit was slowing down. Again, those eyes. I was interested in Mack, not the famous characters who intersected his life. Yet, how could I escape questions about the how and whys of those meetings? Let's focus on Mack, but where to start? In the beginning,

Texas.

Mack confirmed a few things with yes, no, or short answers, very short answers. Yes, he was born in West. Yes, he attended school there. Yes, *Gumbo* was autobiographical. Yes, the events were real in the book. Leading with closed ended questions was getting me nowhere. What was it like playing baseball professionally? "Well we travelled around Texas and Oklahoma, it was hot." Then silence - - - one thousand one, one thousand two, one thousand three, the moments ticked off. I was panicking. I asked another question. What team did you play for? "Dennison Twins and Cardinals I believe." One thousand one, one thousand two, one thousand three. And you played pitcher? "Yes." Damn, I am the worst interviewer. As I was feeling really stupid, Mack must have taken pity and mentioned he played in the Air Force. How did you come to be playing baseball in the Air Force? "I was an athletic instructor. I taught all the team sports, baseball, football, basketball. We mostly played teams from around the base or from other branches." All of my follow up questions were met with a simple "I don't remember" or "I guess." Irina was trying to help, but this was an area of Mack's life that she too was ignorant of. In fact, many of the areas I wanted to talk about was well before she met Mack and not something he felt was important to talk about. Mack offered the key.

"I was never about being famous or a celebrity."

Why?

"It was too time consuming."

My attempts to have him expand failed. I tried probing a couple different ways and was met with a shrug of the shoulders, or silence. "It was too time consuming" was going to stand on its own. I was a little frustrated, I felt there was something important there that I was not finding. Eventually I came to the belief that Mack left that for me to discover so I might better understand him. I would have liked a few hours and a glass of beer to ponder the meaning, but at that moment I was left with Mack not wishing to be a celebrity. Where to go next. With beads of nervous sweat forming on my brow I thought of Paris. Paris with Burroughs was to be my highlight conversation, saved until I had greater rapport. Instead it would hopefully turn my interview around and back into something more positive.

When I began asking him about his music Mack explained that it was his mother who got him interested in music. She would take him to church and he enjoyed the music. He first learned to play the reed instruments such as the clarinet and saxophone. After looking over my notes for inspiration and not finding it, I abruptly switched topics.

"How did you happen to be in Paris?"

"I wanted to play some Jazz. I was bored. Paris sounded interesting."

In what I learned to be true understated Mack Thomas style, Mack went on to talk a little bit about Paris and his time there as a writer and jazz musician. When I asked Mack if he was living in the "Beat Hotel" with Burroughs, he quickly said "No. That place was a dump. I was staying at a much nicer place across the street." He almost seemed insulted by the thought of him living somewhere so run down and cheap. He went on to describe the jazz scene in Paris. American jazz musicians were held in very high esteem and Mack soon took his place among the biggest names.

As a jazz musician, Mack's hours were the opposite of the writers and artists he was spending time with. Often times he would be coming home from all night jam sessions as Burroughs and his crowd were waking up. Mack discussed how Burroughs would be sipping coffee, a drink that Mack hates, while Mack enjoyed a glass of wine. Mack enjoyed travelling the Saint-Germain-des-Pres neighborhood of Paris. At the time it was the hangout for jazz musicians and it attracted large crowds. Mack was receiving more and more acclaim for his unconventional style. While calling his playing "average" he also mentioned that people would come to see him play. He had an encyclopedic memory and could play a vast backlog of tunes. This led him from the smaller, less prestigious basement clubs to nicer and nicer clubs. This was earning him a nice salary in sharp contrast to the writers and other artists who were scrambling and hustling to keep a roof over their heads, and food and drink flowing. Soon Mack was playing tenor saxophone alongside headliners such as Miles Davis, Thelonious Monk, Gene Harris, and Gerry Mulligan. Mack recalled how these jazz leaders would allow Mack the musical room to "improvise and play off the wall and out of the blue." Later Mack would meet up with these same musicians all over the world, from Paris to New Mexico.

After leaving Paris, Mack played the top clubs in New York such as the Five Spot Cafe while living as he said it "in SoHo before it was hip. When it was industrial and empty at night." His list of friends and places he turns up makes him seem like the fictional character Forrest Gump. He recalled being at a New York party and meeting John F. Kennedy at a beach house but could not provide many details about the occasion. As Mack shrugged his shoulders indicating that there was nothing more he remembered, Irina mentioned Mack enjoyed the jazz at El Meson restaurant, a club there in Santa Fe.

Jim Metcalf had mentioned that if I was in Santa Fe on a Friday I needed to attend a jazz club with Mack. Throughout his life Mack always had his table at clubs, this was no different. The second time he attended El Meson, Metcalf said people were sitting at the table Mack felt was now his. After speaking to the manager, the table was made available and for the next few years every Friday night Mack would hold court there. He said "the jazz was generally good, but uninspired," and that the musicians "played it safe too often." I suppose that would be natural for someone who played and listen to the greats in his heyday. It was easy for me to imagine Mack and

Irina dressing for the concert at their favorite club. With Mack's aversion to celebrity I wondered if he ever told the musicians there about his background. I asked if Mack ever sat in and Irina explained that Mack's health kept him from doing that.

Music seems to be how Mack paid his bills wherever he was living. While in Germany he remembered playing the saxophone and sometimes the piano in a quartet. He also lived in Spain and Puerto Rico for short times, always playing jazz. I asked if there are any recordings of him playing. His reply was, "Not with my name on it" and left it at that. He has also combined his musical knowledge with his writing. He has written liner notes for various jazz albums and his columns for Grove Press centered around jazz. As a columnist and critic, Mack was able to find a writing style that he said "did not hitchhike on someone else's talent" while allowing him to "only write about what he liked." His comments about writing led to us discussing his writing career.

When I mentioned his writing Mack opened up by repeating that he didn't want to be a celebrity, it was too time consuming. He gave Allen Ginsberg as an example. Mack's impressions of Ginsberg that he was always out promoting himself or his friends to the determent of Ginsberg's own writing career. Irina recalled hearing that Ginsberg had taken one of Mack's poems and had it published in Germany in a magazine that featured up and coming American Beat writers. Although he wasn't certain Mack believed the publication might have been titled Kulture.

The celebrity nature of being a writer never sat well with Mack. He mentioned several readings in New York that highlighted how negatively he felt those situations were. He recalls arriving at one such gathering that was organized to hear him read, after being asked to tell about his work he answered, "I don't know what to say," then left after collecting his check. He also mentioned feeling sorry for Ernest

Hemingway, a writer whom he mentioned as influencing his own writing. I asked him why he felt sorry for Hemingway, and Mack responded, "because the publicity of Hemingway's life overshadowed everything else." Pressed for details Mack thought for a little while before shrugging his shoulders. Everything else seemed to be about Hemingway's writings, but I can't be certain what Mack was thinking. Later when I asked about any other authors who influenced him, Mack replied, "I don't know." He seemed to forget he mentioned Hemingway.

I asked Mack which writers he enjoyed. "Anything by Mailer," he said. I was a little surprised by his answer. Mack explained, "we met in New York when we did a reading at a woman's house. She was a patron of sorts in the 1970s." Mack continued explaining that he viewed Mailer as a "pro" but a bit of a "bon vivant." Metcalf had told me a different view of Mailer and Mack. Mack had mentioned that at a private book party to celebrate *The Total Beast* Mailer had sulked in the corner because he believed Mack would be stealing some of the spotlight from his novels.

Mack quickly ran through a couple of names without revealing many details. He enjoyed Gregory Corso's work. He said he was closer to Corso in Paris than many other authors and felt he knew Corso better than anyone else in town. While Mack's name comes up in several books and articles, I had not seen him associated with Corso. Mack also liked Jack Kerouac's writing but did not remember if they had met. "Probably I guess, we had the same friends." William Faulkner was another well-known author whose name found its way to the top reaches of Mack's memory. Running out of things to discuss I turned to Mack's own writing.

I started with his childhood and asked about his family's reading habits. He mentioned his dad, who was a cotton mill employee, was a reader. His answer to my question about having books in his house growing up, was a shrug of the shoulders and the comment, "I guess." He did remember that reading was his escape and he spent time lying on the living room floor reading. He could not remember what he enjoyed reading, but Jim Metcalf mentioned in an email that Mack read a lot of history books, that nonfiction seemed to be his favorite genre. Our conversation on his writing jumped from one area to another, from being a columnist to being a writer of novels.

Starting with his novels, he affirmed that *Gumbo* and *The Total Beast* were autobiographical. However, like most publishers of the time, it was a requirement that Mack not use real names, not even his own. Mack writing two autobiographical novels was very interesting. I asked him why he chose to write autobiographical novels, his answer made me chuckle, "Because it was easy! I wanted to write about something I knew." Later in a follow up interview I asked him why, as a private person wishing to protect his anonymity, why he would write something so personal. Again he fell back on it as being easy and further explaining he "never wanted to work too hard." This leads to a curious quote of Mack's that his friends remember: "If at first you don't succeed, quit."

Mack believes that you are either good at something, or you are not. Why waste time on something that you do not do well, and miss out on the things that you do well? If you are good at something you will know right away. As an educator myself, I have been taught to persevere, to keep trying. I hear the tired clichés that winners never quit and quitters never win. But I was sitting across from someone who had quit and won. At 86 years young he was leading a life that few people will ever live. Mack allowed himself to follow his interests which he described as "mostly curiosity, not specialized." He added that he had "broad interests, and was not dumb." He had many careers, but each career allowed him to work anywhere and to follow his passions. That might not have happened if he stayed a dance instructor or continued his diaper service. I believe he is right.

Returning to Mack's novels, I began thinking about what I

had already learned from Jim Metcalf's e-mails. "Mack wrote *The Total Beast* in a house about a mile downstream from where he built his house (El Rito). This was an old house with board and batten exterior shaped in a U . . . the cross of the U was the living room. (It) had a fireplace and dirt floor covered in flagstone...had not been mortared. He wrote 16 hours a day for four years on the book."

If he wrote 16 hours a day, that was far from easy in my mind. I also knew that there were Hollywood aspirations for *The Total Beast*. Again from an email from Jim Metcalf:

In 1971 Mack came to LA to peddle *The Total Beast* to Hollywood to make a movie. He stayed with me in my one bedroom apt, as he had no money. He had not yet written the screenplay and I took him to meet a woman I knew who was Ross Hunter's executive secretary. She had selected *Airport* and brought it to his (Ross Hunter's) attention. She asked if he had ever written a screenplay before and he said no, and she asked how long he thought it would take and he said, about 6 weeks and she essentially laughed at him. He hooked up with George Peppard, who was doing "Banacek" at the time and his stock was high.

The next time Mack came to LA, Paramount put him up in a suite at the Sportsman's Lodge in the valley and gave him an expense account. He was doing screenplay rewrites on a movie Peppard was making, "Newman's Law", a cops and robbers movie. Nobody knows more about cops and robbers than Mack. Before he left, Paramount offered him a job producing a TV show.

Then things turned sour for Mack and Hollywood. From Metcalf's email:

The announcement actually came out in the entertainment section of the LA Times Sunday paper that Peppard's next movie would be *The Total Beast*. He tried to renegotiate the contract and pissed people off and they told him to go fuck himself and the project was killed.

Mack stayed around and did some things with Paramount and called me one day at the hospital and said he was leaving LA and would never be back. They were trying to steal all his ideas and fuck him. Even though he was poor, and had no money at the time, he was unwilling to compromise and left Hollywood and never came back.

Looking across the small space that separated us I could see the type of determination that allowed him to tell Hollywood no.

Mack shrugged his shoulders and did not seem to remember many of the details that Metcalf had shared. However, he did remember one thing, and he remembered it very vividly about his time in Hollywood and the attempt to have *The Total Beast* made into a movie. When I asked him what he thought of having George Peppard play him on the big screen, he leaned forward and in a clear voice said "George Peppard is an asshole!" That ended the discussion of *The Total Beast* and Hollywood.

Not so surprisingly when pressed about his writing career, Mack said, "I never thought of myself as a good writer." Then when I asked what critics thought of his writing, he replied that "(he) did not read any reviews." I asked him for the events surrounding having his two novels published. He mentioned that he was asked to write both novels. Grove Press, where he was working as an editor and columnist, published *Gumbo* and Simon and Schuster, the top publisher at that time, had approached him about *The Total Beast*. He described Grove Press as being much less formal than Simon and Schuster. Mack's aversion to being a celebrity and his desire for privacy made him a publicist's nightmare. He did no interviews, made no appearances, and never autographed a book. Metcalf said Mack wanted the book to stand on its own. There was some publicity for *Gumbo* which had been excerpted in the *Saturday*

Evening Post. Clay Felker, the editor of the *Saturday Evening Post,* liked Mack's work and prominently placed it in the magazine. Felker was not the only well-known editor of the day to appreciate Mack's work.

Fred Jordan at Grove Press hired Mack and was someone who Mack "enjoyed working with." Jordan eventually served twenty years as Grove's Editor-in-Chief. Mack worked both as an editor and columnist for Grove. This lead to Mack "reading a lot of their stuff (Beat writers)" but "not having a lot of strong feelings about their work." Mack stuck to reviewing things he liked which were "cerebrally intelligent" and without "frivolity." He also appreciated authors who "had experiences by going afield" and "who took chances" in their writing.

How Mack came to be employed at Grove Press was going to touch on a subject that I was fearing to tread, Mack's time in prison. One of the terms of his parole from the Texas prison system was that he find a job and leave the state. He had been writing some pieces for Grove while serving his time. One theory is that part of Mack's troubles in jail and what may have placed him in the solitary confinement "shitter" (a 4' x 4' x 4' windowless concrete box), was a check from Grove to Mack. Writing while in prison was against the rules. When asked about prison, Mack was polite but firm in his response, "Prison does not have a significant place in my brain." To fill in some important gaps not covered in *The Total Beast*, we are left with some educated guesses from people who asked me not to reveal their names out of respect for Mack.

From the stories I have been told, Mack's release was orchestrated in part with strong political connections. Many of his friends, probably including the *Saturday Evening Post* folks at Evergreen Press, had been quietly petitioning politicians in Texas and Washington to intervene. *Gumbo* had been serialized in the *Saturday Evening Post* which brought Mack acclaim. The New York publishing community pushed New York Senator Jacob Javitz to contact the Governor of

Texas and let him know the best literary mind in America was in Huntsville on a marijuana charge. It was his friend's hard work, combined with expectations of Mack's future literary contributions, that came together to have him paroled. After five years and three months in a Texas prison, Mack now found himself a free man. Because Mack was not as well known outside New York, it was probably easier to work the system and have him released. His next challenge was being penniless in Texas and needing to get to New York in 48 hours to accept a job. But in true Mack fashion he hitchhiked across the country and soon found himself living in New York. He explained with a hint of anger in his voice that his thoughts rarely returned to Texas during that time.

Mack was getting tired. We had talked for several hours and Mack excused himself to go to bed. Marvilyn and I began to gather our journals when Irina invited us to stay and have a light dinner with her. We accepted her gracious offer. The next couple of questions from Irina were easy to answer: Do you like red or white wine and do you like caviar? Red, and yes. Irina had also made a Russian dish similar to a ragout that was exquisite. The Alaskan caviar was served on crisp homemade bread crackers. Again this was not what I was expecting. We chatted for more than an hour. Irina may have asked more questions than I did. We did learn about her artwork, especially the woodcuts she creates. We made plans to drive to El Rito the next day. It was getting late. We wrapped things up and said our goodbyes.

The drive back to our hotel was filled with exclamations of disbelief as we discussed the questions and answers we heard from both Irina and Mack during and after the interview. Soon we were back to the hotel and thinking about tomorrow.

Mack Thomas The Total Beat

EL RITO, NEW MEXICO

We arrived on time and rang the doorbell. Irina was ready to go and the caregiver for Mack had arrived. We exchanged small talk with Mack and soon made our way down the hallway to the back door. We were standing in the driveway as the garage door opened. Inside were two gleaming white late model Mercedes Benz. Irina backed the SUV from the garage and we were off to El Rito. Irina was the perfect hostess and tour guide as we maneuvered through Santa Fe traffic and out to the countryside. Our conversation turned to Mack and I asked her how they met. She laughed a bit as she started the story.

Her husband had passed away tragically many months before and her friends had been urging her to date. Mack was without a steady girlfriend and his friends were urging him to get out more. Naturally both sets of friends secretly created online profiles for Mack and Irina on a popular dating site without each of them knowing. Later Mack and Jim Metcalf began scanning profiles and pictures when they found Irina's. Soon Irina was receiving a lot of messages from Mack who was above all - persistent.

Eventually she was captivated and agreed to a date. She decided to invite Mack to a dinner party she was hosting for a few friends. During the dinner party Irina had shown the guests around her home. Mack has a keen eye for details and the next day, as a thank you to the hostess, he had a luxurious bed sent to Irina as a little gift. Irina went on to explain that she was using a small platform bed that was just perfect for her. I asked what her reaction was to receive a bed as a gift. Irina replied she was surprised. However, in hearing the story I was not surprised. It actually seemed like a normal thing for Mack to do. There was, however, one lingering issue from the dating site profile. When Mack's friends created his profile, they had shaved a few years off of Mack's real age, actually they shaved off over a decade. Irina is no fool, and possesses the wisdom that a woman develops after dating a few men. Yet, he easily passed for a man much younger than his years. Was it his eyes?

As we headed north Irina told stories of how important El Rito was to Mack. This was the place that Mack had chosen to get away from it all. This is, in many ways, more of a glimpse into Mack's life than the questions I was asking. He built this with his own hands, this was his retreat from the world. The who, what, when, where, and why of this place reveal a lot about Mack.

It was easy to see why Mack found solitude in El Rito. Santa Fe is not a large city to begin with and we were driving a couple hours north. We had left the interstate and began moving through areas that city lovers would call the middle of nowhere with nothing to see. I was glad I was not driving. I was able to enjoy the rolling hills and mountains, the forests and the few small towns we passed. Despite it being March, winter was clinging to the upper elevations. Snow was visible further up. Irina had warned us to pack warm clothes and boots in case the cabin was still covered in snow. The cold outside was in sharp contrast to the warmth in the car. Irina's story was every bit as interesting as Mack's.

Irina was born in Russia and after briefly settling in

Europe, she came to the United States where she was a successful businessperson in Houston, Texas. On a vacation to Santa Fe, she met a young beekeeper and fell in love. After attempting a long distance romance he drove to Houston with a moving truck, asked her to move to Santa Fe, and the Houston population dropped by one. It seems that men take bold actions after meeting Irina. One man surprised her with a moving truck and another felt that a luxurious bed was a suitable thank you gift to the hostess of a dinner party.

After spending a few days and sharing many emails with Irina, it was clear that she deserved a fairy tale romance. However, that was not to be. Tragically her bee keeper partner passed away suddenly. With a number of options, she decided to stay in Santa Fe. She is such a wonderful hostess that I hesitate to talk too much about her, but I believe by understanding her a little bit, you can better understand Mack.

Mack has had many ladies in his life. No one really knows for certain how many, perhaps Mack probably doesn't even remember. There is a mysterious lady friend in *The Total Beast* who remains an enigma. His female personal assistant, who works from his and Irina's home, is a former lover. His friends tell stories of how women have always been attracted to Mack. Irina confesses that the number of Mack's former lovers make Santa Fe at times uncomfortable. She has learned to maneuver in those moments when she is face to face with one of those former lovers. Mack seems to have a knack of keeping those ladies as friends. During my interview with Mack, he mentioned he preferred "bright, intelligent, and attractive women". Based on the lady friends we met or heard about, that may have been a slight understatement.

Irina is not ordinary. I could have easily been an art critic writing an article about her work instead of Mack's life. While she apologizes about her English, she communicates very well, with a polished ease. Even while casually dressed she carries herself with a quiet confidence and elegance. It is easy to see how some men may be intimidated by her. I share Jim Metcalf's belief that few people on the planet can match Mack's intelligence. However, Irina has his undivided attention and can hold up her end of a conversation. Looking across the car seat, I believe Irina seems like the perfect woman for Mack. After about two hours of steady driving and talking we passed a sign noting that El Rito was 5 miles further. As we continued winding through the mountains I thought that El Rito was probably more a general area than a specific dot on the map. Eventually we arrived in the town.

The town was a couple of blocks long, with buildings lining both sides of the dusty street. There were more broken windows than intact ones. Half the town was boarded up, the other half looked like it was waiting for the boards. Locals describe the town in a self-depreciating way as the cheerful ruins. There was one business open and busy, El Farolito Restaurant. In a town that was all faded and rotting wood, surprisingly, Irina's Mercedes looked right at home outside the old restaurant. We parked next to a Land Rover with the dealer tag still on the back window, a Volvo with Texas plates, and an old Ford that may, or more likely may not be, in running condition with expired tags. Irina offered an enthusiastic endorsement of the restaurant, telling us we will love the food. A closer inspection of the restaurant's front causes me to think this was drawn by a child whose box of crayons was missing all the bright colors. There is a door in the middle with two windows evenly spaced on both sides. Despite the artist's best efforts to make the building seem cheerful, the outside blended in with the rest of the town.

We entered the door and everyone turned with anticipation of knowing who was walking through the door. The owner knew Irina and asked about Mack. I began to sense that Mack was a celebrity in this town. If this was the town's best restaurant, Mack would have been coming here for decades. Still the concerned look and hushed tones from the owner made it seem that Mack was more than a popular customer. Later I learned of the positive economic impact that Mack had had on the town for a brief spell.

Living in the Rio Grande Valley along the Texas border with Mexico, my wife and I know our way around a small Mexican cash-only type restaurant. Being in New Mexico we began thinking about green chilies. The restaurant was almost full with only one repurposed kitchen table and mismatched chairs available to us. I suspect that even if every table was being used that this was the kind of place where other diners would make room for you at their tables. As steaming plates of red, green, or "Christmas" chili- covered plates left the kitchen, lively conversations were replaced by smiles and enthusiastic eating.

When Irina returned she mentioned that the owner was interested in how Mack was doing, when he would be returning, and wanted Irina to send good wishes back to Mack. Plans to reunite in Santa Fe were tentatively set. It was easy to see that Mack was a local. Mack had talked about having "his table" back at jazz clubs in Santa Fe. He probably had a favorite table here as well. Before I could ask Irina the question, our food arrived and our thoughts were simply about the food. Describing the food seems like a pointless activity now; suffice to say we will return next time we are in the neighborhood. And in this case the neighborhood is defined as being within a couple hundred miles. Back "in town", El Farolito would be a five- star, must-stop, on the culinary tour with double or triple the menu prices. Instead they are the local diner. Location is everything.

Location is why Mack first bought property in El Rito back in 1967. Mack was looking for a secluded place where he could be himself without authorities and neighbors bothering him. He certainly found it there in El Rito. With each turn off from yet another road to reach a smaller road which led to an even smaller road, which then went from pavement to gravel, we inched closer to Mack's retreat. Old was being replaced by new.

Modern structures were popping up and replacing some of the trailer homes that we passed. The people who could afford second homes were buying the land that other people called their first homes. I wondered where the old time residents went after they sold their land. Did they buy land further into the mountains? Move to the city to find jobs? Or were they just down the road working for the new residents? Probably all of the above.

We passed what I thought was Mack's hand built cabin. I was mistaken. Irina explained that was a studio and apartment that Mack allowed some visitors to use. One artist-in-residence was also one of Mack's lovers. He allowed her to stay and develop her art during the day. She would visit the main cabin in the evening, and retreat to the studio at night. This was perfectly aligned with Mack's desire for privacy. If Mack was to ever write another book, a 'how to romance ladies guide' would certainly serve mankind well. Jim Metcalf had mentioned in his emails to me a couple of times that Mack was amazing around the ladies. This was confirmed with each new story that Irina told.

After driving across a small creek we reached the cabin Mack built. Clearly everyone was stretching the definition of a cabin. This was far more polished and larger than what most people call a cabin. I remember being on Mount Desert Island in Acadia National Park in Maine and hearing locals call the estate homes of the Rockefeller set "cottages." Tucked up next to a hillside, this Midwestern boy could clearly see a Frank Lloyd Wright inspired design. Low slung, the rock and wood structure fit perfectly into the surroundings. Metcalf listed architect along with Mack's other talents and I would agree. If a structure could be crouching to hide, this cabin was clearly trying to not take away the beauty of the land that surrounded it. I wasn't certain what I was expecting, but from the design to the size, this was not in my vision.

We parked and stood outside in the crisp air and I

immediately felt the peace and serenity of the land. Wilderness travel has been one of my favorite activities. With my wife and a couple of backpacks I find serenity. In nature I find a certain quietness that also quiets my brain. I usually do not find that next to a driveway and a large home. But here I could. The air was crisp and fresh, the ground seemed to be vibrant and alive beneath our feet even with snow crunching under our boots.

Mack's health has kept him and Irina from visiting El Rito on a regular basis. This trip would give her a chance to check on the condition of the property, relax a bit at a favorite place, and help me to gain a better understanding of Mack. Looking at the cabin I estimated the size of Mack's retreat at over 2,000 square feet. The grounds were very neat and tidy. Mack employs a full time caretaker who manages the property. Moises Archuleta, the caretaker had been alerted by Irina that we would be visiting. As we approached the front door I took one more look around the grounds. I was trying to image Mack, William Burroughs, and James Grauerholz hanging out under the trees smoking a joint. Somehow this was not fitting my image of Burroughs. I had vintage photographs of Burroughs in my mind but I just could not fit them into this landscape. It was much easier to insert the dust jacket photo of Mack. Tall and muscular, I could see Mack knocking down trees to shape into beams or carrying heavy stones from the creek to build the fireplace. I always saw Burroughs inside, or in a city. Even knowing that Burroughs had farmed in the Rio Grande Valley of Texas did not help my attempts. I kept seeing Burroughs wearing a hat and trench coat stepping carefully around the muddy spots while Mack blazed a trail. Metcalf had filled me in on a few details in an e-mail.

"I was there before he started building the house in El Rito. It is actually built around a log cabin about 100 years old. That door from the living room to the dining room, was the front door. The dining room was the living room. I went up into the mountains with him close to Taos where there had been some forest fire decades before that had left tall pines that were bare as far as you could see. They were cured and if you hit them with an ax they rang like a bell. He cut down all those logs in the house and trucked them back, and of course he got the huge stones for the fireplace from the stream. I worked on the house with him during my visits as it took a couple of years. He did most of it by himself."

Irina opened the door and we stepped into the living room. Looking around I began studying the workmanship.

Mack had built this home from those local logs that he felled and prepared. This did not look like a makeshift hastily-built cabin; it was easy to see that Metcalf remembered correctly and it would have taken a couple of years to build. The chinking was perfectly symmetrical throughout the home. That requires careful and constant attention to detail. This was a well-designed home built by a master craftsman. Off the living room was a plant-filled sun room with a very prominent fern growing in the middle. Lots of glass doors and windows offered views to the clearing behind the home. The kitchen and main bedroom was also off the living room. As Irina took us on a tour of their slightly softened "man cave," I started to paint a picture of Mack. It starts with the books he had stuffed everywhere.

First there were no show-case books. No books left out to impress. These were books meant to be read and probably had been read. Mack told Metcalf that he had read over 20,000 books in his lifetime. Perhaps ironically Wilt Chamberlain, the National Basketball League star once boasted about having sex with 20,000 different women. I would say that most likely both of those numbers are exaggerated. However, knowing what I know about Mack's life, which admittedly is not very much, if I had to bet that one of those numbers was true, I'm going with Mack's 20,000 books. Scanning the titles there were many volumes about building construction, furniture construction, and the various necessities to build and maintain "El Rito". There were countless books by the Beat Generation authors.

These were mixed in with history, philosophy, art, music, and countless others. Some were stacked on a shelf behind his bed, others were placed on ledges or stacked here and there. I was surprised that there didn't seem to be any organization to them. Based on the order that surrounded Mack at home I expected that he, or an assistant, would have categorized and organized the books. I kept thinking how amazing it would be to not only have read all these great books, but actually have used and understood them. I was tempted to peak in some of the Burroughs' books to see how many were personally inscribed to Mack. Somehow I never got around to asking, or felt it would have been a terrible intrusion to Mack's privacy. I learned the answer after Mack's passing when Irina sent me a photo of Burroughs' "Port of Saints" from 1980 in which Burroughs wrote "For Mack Thomas who has found it / Love / William S Burroughs.

Knowing what a private person Mack is, at first I felt uncomfortable roaming around his house. At times it felt like a museum. My thoughts were broken when Irina asked if we would like a glass of wine. She had brought a snack from El Farolito and was standing with an open bottle of red wine and three glasses. The lady knows how to entertain. After pouring the wine she turned her attention to the fireplace. The caretaker had built a small fire in the large stone fireplace, the only step necessary was to light the tinder. This was spring break but snow was still on the ground here at the higher elevations and the air inside the cabin was slightly chilly. A bottle of wine, snacks, and a fire in the fireplace. I was feeling so much a guest that once again I forgot I was there to interview Irina about Mack. As we sat and shared the bottle of wine, Irina shared some El Rito stories. Most of the stories would be second hand from things Mack and his friends shared with her. Mack's friends are careful what they share, both out of respect to Mack's privacy and to Irina's feelings. It may be possible to draw an opinion that Mack is hiding something or worried about confrontation. That is not the case. His friends all say he is honest and straightforward. He would sooner tell you he was not going to answer than fake forgetting.

The first story started when Irina spotted what looked to be a purse hanging by the door. Mack was an inventor and back in the 1960s he invented the "Love Mitt" which he sold through Neiman Marcus and other retailers. Always the romantic, Mack realized that the winter months made it difficult for lovers to stroll along while holding hands. His answer was a long fur-lined tube that two people could reach through and hold hands. We took it down from its peg and Marvilyn and I tried it on. It is similar to today's version of a cross-body purse. There was a strap that went over the shoulder and a pocket to hold small items. As we reached into the mitt to hold hands we shared a smile and a vision of 1960s well-healed lovers holding hands. This was so typically Mack. I was told that the Love Mitt sold well as a unique gift during the holiday season.

I asked about the manufacturing. Mack hired the local people there in El Rito to manufacture the mitt in the "sheep shop." In fact, many people in town remember working for Mack. This fact explained how Mack became so well known in the area. I could imagine most of the town heading to the same factory to cut, sew, and pack Love Mitts. Somehow it was the perfect gift. The dust jacket of Mack's books mentioned a few of his other inventions. No one could remember the chromium plated bug deflector, but they did remember the Safety Tube.

The Safety Tube was a first aid kit and rescue device in one. The sealed plastic container contained items important to survival. Later as we toured some of the out buildings we discovered one of the canisters. Just looking at the contents it would appear that this product was like many before it and many after it. What was different was the care that Mack took in choosing each item. Jim Metcalf mentioned that Mack went to visit a manufacturer of elastic bandages whose product Mack was considering usingin the Safety Tube. He asked the company owner if the elastic bandages were fireproof. The owner thought his product was fireproof, an opinion that Mack proved wrong by lighting a sample on fire in an ashtray.

I still had no clue how Mack amassed his personal fortune. Another possibility is the plastics manufacturing firm that Mack and his brother owned. Mack was able to use the anticipated royalties from his books and his El Rito property as collateral for a start-up loan. Irina mentioned that Mack was more the investor and his brother ran the business. As intelligent and charismatic as Mack is, it was easy for me to accept that he did well in each enterprise and eventually built a nice retirement. It was hard to focus as I continued to survey the rooms to learn all I could about Mack. With his health and memory fading these glimpses would become a big part of framing my understanding of Mack. Who knows which items in the cabin would be significant and which would not? With Mack, sometimes the ordinary everyday items have a story attached. We continued our tour of the cabin.

In the kitchen was a traditional baked bean pot. This one looked handed down from one generation to the other. Irina noticed it caught my eye and explained that Mack owned it with his "English ex-wife." After the divorce she took it with her. Later Mack found he just couldn't live without it. An agreement was made that Mack could keep the bean pot until his death. After his death the pot would be returned to her.

In the bedroom we noticed that Mack had built all of the furniture. The dressers and nightstands were built into the walls. Alcoves were created to store books and other small items. Everything was plumb, every hinge worked smoothly, every bit of joinery was perfect, every detail in place. As Metcalf explained in several emails, Mack does not miss any details with people nor with objects. Each item flowed together in some harmony that Mack had envisioned. We found ourselves wandering from room to room. As we were walking through the sunroom Marvilyn noticed some damage to one of the sofas. It looked as if a large dog or very large cat had clawed or bitten the leather. When Marvilyn asked about the damage, Irina gave a little laugh and told the story.

She and Mack were asleep one night when they heard a commotion in the living room. The house is vacant many days of the year and they immediately assumed someone had broken in who did not notice their car in the driveway. Mack reached for the handgun he kept in the bedroom and they carefully opened the bedroom door expecting to see the person who had broken in. Instead a bear had broken in and was looking for whatever bears would be looking for in a cabin. They quickly retreated into the bedroom and closed the door. Mack understood that his handgun was no match for this large bear. In fact, attempting to shoot the bear would result in a wounded and much more dangerous bear. There is no phone service at the cabin. Basically they huddled in the room and waited for the bear to leave. When the bear left Mack began plans for a security upgrade to the cabin. Burglar bars were placed on the windows near the back of the house.

The cabin is built right up against the hillside. A low wall, perhaps three feet in height, runs along the back of the cabin. Irina mentioned a time when she watched a bear with cubs walk calmly along the wall peering into the windows. It was a bit comical to me thinking of this well-mannered artist a few feet from a wild bear with Mack as the common denominator. Irina suggested we take a walk around the property to visit the workshop, guest house, and an old school site. I was still wondering about the bears.

As we walked around the property, I was being extra careful in spotting any wildlife. We didn't see any bears. It was spring and foraging away from humans was how bears were earning their living. We were stepping on the snow that was still ankle deep in the shady areas. As we neared the guest house we could hear the creek that ran between the two houses. Standing on the small bridge I viewed the creek both as a physical and a metaphorical barrier between Mack and the outside world. I was still trying to reconcile Mack's contention that he is a private person with the man who always has his table inside a club. The man who wrote two autobiographical novels. The man who by most accounts had many friends, several close friends he shared deep thoughts. Perhaps it was not his privacy he was guarding all along. It may have been he was guarding his time with himself. This is a man who enjoys ideas. He is a careful planner and an even more careful executioner. He didn't need other people's praise and acknowledgement because earning his own was such a high standard and much more rewarding. He challenged himself to a greater degree than the outside world would ever challenge him. As we stepped off the bridge I turned to look back at the cabin and noticed that even in the early spring the cabin was barely visible from the guest house.

The artwork in the guest house was striking to this non artist. I could almost feel the creative energy that had walked and created in these rooms. There were many gifts left behind by the appreciative guests. Had this been the cabin that Mack built, it would have been an impressive feat in its own right. Large and airy with plenty of sunshine for writing or painting, it seems like the ideal place to hole up and complete a dream. I imagine staying here was a special invitation that was treasured by Mack's friends. Mack also used this as an office. Irina explained in an email that "Mack had several women living in El Rito in the studio, which was called 'an office' before my time. One of them lived there for seven years, another for four years. They were his lovers in the beginning - friends, book keepers and secretaries after some time (they even call themselves 'slaves', laughingly) … After divorcing his English wife, he had a lot of lovers, but maintained his bachelor status for thirty years, until he met me." Irina wasn't really certain what all he was working on while he was spending work time here. Perhaps it was tied to the manufacturing of the Love Mitt. Irina took a few minutes looking around and making notes on repairs and improvements that needed to be made. After she was satisfied that everything had been taken care of we made our way to the door.

After leaving the guesthouse we headed over to the workshop and a chance to meet Mack's long time caretaker of the property. Irina had sent me this in an email about Moises Archuleta. "Mack met him when he was 19 and they worked together ever since... Mack taught Moises all the skills of a builder, carpenter, plumber, mason...you name it. Sometimes they both learned on the job, doing things, not liking it, demolishing, starting again. Moises knows how to install technologically complex things just from their manuals, which is still fascinating to me." As we talked I raised my foot, resting my boot upon the lower boards of the fence and looked out over Mack and Irina's property.

The workshop was next to the corrals where a couple of horses were shaking off the cold and watching us with disinterested eyes. Moises had opened the large overhead doors and was making himself busy. Irina introduced Marvilyn and myself to Moises and explained why I was there. Moises appears to be in his fifties or early sixties, fit from years of hard work. I sensed Moises becoming guarded. As a lifelong employee of Mack's, he knew Mack's desire for privacy and was probably calculating what he should and more importantly should not say to me. As Irina and Moises made small talk I began to realize how little Irina knew about Mack's history compared to others around him. Based on how guarded Mack's friends are about Mack and the complexity of his life, I doubt Irina will ever know more than the very tip of Mack's life. At times this seemed to me that Irina appeared as an outsider in her own home. Often she seemed to be as interested in knowing the answers to my questions as I was. Or perhaps it was her polite manners.

Each time Irina asked Moises a question or made a request I

sensed he was conflicted. I guessed he would have been much more comfortable if it was Mack and not Irina making the request. I tried to get him to tell some stories of the property and the events that happened here, but at each step he was very measured in his responses. I looked around for something to talk about. The building was neat and well organized with a lot of items stored around. We found a Safety Tube that had never been opened. We opened it and each item looked like it still could be used in an emergency. Tools looked as if they were ready to begin construction on a new building at any moment. Because Mack had not visited on a regular basis in recent months there was not much need for maintenance.

I asked Moises about the workshop. He explained that the building was not always a workshop. Located a several hundred yards from the main house, Mack originally used it to build the main house and everything that went inside. Later it was used as a makeshift concert venue and dance hall. Moises described how Mack would invite everyone in the area every Sunday to come by and play their instruments, drink, dance, and share a potluck dinner.

The day before, Mack had remembered a few details about those events. I noted that a smile crept across his face as he spoke about playing with that crowd. He said the music was good because they "had a good piano there" but the music eventually suffered because "nobody practiced enough." It was an open mic performance and anyone could take the stage and play. There were mostly impromptu groups jamming or adapting the latest music to fit their style. I thought back to the owner of El Farolito and continued to understand Mack's role in the town. He brought jobs and entertainment to the community. I wondered if Mack preferred playing in a hip Paris jazz club with Miles Davis, New York clubs with Thelonious Monk, or headlining an open mic in his barn. I believe the venue did not matter, that what mattered was the music and his own performance. I think he could have been perfectly content to play with anyone and without any audience. In a later email Irina offered this glimpse into Mack's life in El Rito and his relationship to the community:

"Moises told me that, even when Mack lived there, he would suddenly disappear for a long periods of time, writing... Mack did not encourage locals to come to visit him casually and kept very few friends in El Rito. He used to not have any weapons or dogs at first. During Roy's (Mack's brother) visit, an arsonist lit fires under several houses in El Rito, including Mack's wood shop. Nothing happened, the smoldering rug was discovered in time, but Roy gave Mack his Winchester rifle (he recently took it back) and Mack got his first dog, Wag, a Golden Retriever. Since then, Mack kept a carry-weapon permit. We drove to Dallas in the summer of 2008 to renew it and Mack passed the shooting exam one month before his 80th Birthday. Mack was somewhat feared and respected in El Rito.

I certainly could understand anyone feeling fearful of Mack. He had served time in prison and was notably a tough guy. With his intelligence and creativity, I could see him being respected in this small town.

Returning to my conversation with Moises, I asked about Burroughs' visit to El Rito. At first Burroughs' name did not ring a bell with Moises. I added what little facts I knew and a little of what Mack remembered. This helped Moises to remember the visit. He was not too impressed with Burroughs or the friend he had with him (James Grauerholz). In fact, he found Burroughs to be a bore. But he remembered that Mack was very excited about the visit and Mack and Burroughs would have long conversations each day. Moises didn't remember much about the conversations except that the conversations did not seem to be much about anything. But he knew that Mack really enjoyed spending time with his old friend. I was disappointed I was not learning more about the Burroughs' visit.

I was still thinking of Mack as a literary figure. Later, as I pulled my research together to begin writing, my view of Mack began to center around music and literature. There is probably a story about Mack's business success that needs to be written.

Irina was trying to help my interview of Moises by asking Moises about things she knew. She asked Moises about the manufacturing of the Love Mitt. Many of Moises's family had worked producing the product. He said that almost everyone he knew helped at one time or another. My background was in manufacturing, and this helped me realize that Mack was ahead of the manufacturing curve with this operation.

Mack had a low tech product which needed low tech manufacturing. Sewing machines and the skills to run them had not changed much in a hundred years. The skills could be taught quickly and most people could master those skills in a short time. By locating in El Rito, Mack had a sizable workforce spread out around the area that was ready and willing to work. Being a community insider, Mack was trusted and respected. Mack was in production with a very small footprint and a small investment in materials. Later, when demand eased, Mack would downsize and eventually close the business without huge losses. The same process is used today with production outsourced to companies located in low wage areas.

Irina was the first to mention a three drawer filing cabinet in the middle of the room. I had asked Mack the day before where his papers were stored. Mack was not certain but Annie, his secretary, believed they were in a filing cabinet at El Rito. Irina asked Moises if he had a key to that cabinet. Moises was not certain and looked around. After a few minutes of looking we gave up and returned to our conversation and tour.

There are ruins of an old abandoned schoolhouse located on Mack's property. We left the workshop and hiked to the spot. Moises tried to explain the boundaries of Mack's property. The boundaries tell a tale of Mack's relationships and financial history. He had bought and sold several parcels that surrounded his cabin. This land we were walking towards was part of a settlement with his ex-wife. The negotiations of the settlement allowed Mack a unique right to approve the next owner of the property and the right of first refusal. After meeting the person who would be Mack's neighbor (neighbor in the sense of being about a half mile away), Mack decided to buy back the property himself.

We walked down the driveway a few hundred yards to the road, then through a several fields to reach the ruins. All that remained was a stone floor and most of the fireplace. Rotting boards with old nails were strewn around the site. Marvilyn found a hand forged horseshoe that is now a treasured artifact from our trip. There was some discussion about what may come of the land, but for now it is another buffer between Mack and the outside world.

As we slowly made our way back to the cabin the conversations began to fade. I was alone with my thoughts which turned to Mack Thomas of *Gumbo* and *The Total Beast*. If a Hollywood producer wished to make a movie version of *Gumbo*, the producer could easily use El Rito as the location for Mack's childhood home. Mack had built a physical and mental retreat from the world. I could imagine the school principal growing grapes over the next hill. I could imagine Toby's grandfather living in town. Even the time frame of *Gumbo*, the Great Depression, would fit with the current condition of the town of El Rito. For the inmate who had no choices, this house allowed Mack to make his own rules and set his own schedule. I knew our visit was coming to an end and I was happy with all I saw. We said our goodbyes to Moises and continued on to the cabin.

At the cabin Irina cleaned up a bit from our visit, checked that the fire was out, and began closing up. I headed to the restroom. As I turned on the light I noticed a number of golf trophies. I had forgotten that Metcalf had once told me that Mack was a very avid golfer. When Mack would winter in Palm

Springs he would play golf with Don Meredith and President Ford. He was also a regular dinner guest at Dinah Shore's home. On the toilet tank sat several golf trophies from Mission Hills Country Club. A few pictures of Mack playing golf were hanging on the walls. I was thinking that most people would have these pictures hanging in a prominent spot in their homes. For Mack, these pictures and trophies were regulated to the bathroom as an afterthought.

I rejoined the group in the kitchen as Irina made her final inspection. With one more look around I followed Irina out the door and we walked to the car. I wish Mack had been able to join us that day. I tried my best to wipe the mud from my boots as I got into the car and closed the door.

Irina decided to take a different route back to the highway. We passed the town's library and Irina asked if we would like to stop in to have a look around. Of course we stopped. The building was one of the newer buildings we saw in town, probably less than ten years old and well maintained. The circulation desk was in the foyer and rooms branched off to either side. Irina knew everyone there and was engaged in quiet conversation while Marvilyn and I looked around. I check the database to see if either or both of Mack's books were part of their collection. They were not. Irina introduced me to the librarian and briefly described my project. The librarian had no idea that Mack was an author or had any ties to other authors. She promised to locate copies of Mack's books to circulate. I did not want to stop her efforts so I did not mention how difficult finding a library version was going to be. Irina made promises to be back soon and we left for the drive back to Santa Fe. A few months later she sent me this email:

"We are going to El Rito today; Mack is feeling so much better there. In Santa Fe, he sleeps almost all day.

I told him — 'You seem to be much perkier in El Rito.'

- 'Well, I have nothing to do in Santa Fe, but lay on my ass all day.'

- 'But isn't that what you do in El Rito, anyway?'

- 'No, there I look around and see every log I brought from the forest, every flagstone I dug from the side of the mountain, every boulder I rolled from the river to build the fireplace... It's not the same!'

Mack has an almost mystic connection to the land he purchased back in 1967, almost 50 years ago.

COMING HOME

The next day Marvilyn and I returned to Mack's home with a few more questions. Mack was tired and asked if we would join him in his bedroom. Irina, Marvilyn, and I sat down and we started chatting. Mack asked us about our trip to El Rito, what we thought of the town, and his place. I looked around and saw the usual struggles with health issues. Pill bottles, glasses of water, and books by today's popular authors.

We really did not discuss anything of substance. I was thinking how much I would have enjoyed meeting him ten, twenty, or thirty years earlier. I asked him about the file cabinet left in the workshop in El Rito and if it contained his old papers. With a shrug he said, "if you say so." The key was found several months later, but by then everyone was busy and the contents would have to wait for another day. The only hint I have about the cabinet's contents are from a couple of Mack's poems that Jim Metcalf and Irina shared with me. Both mentioned how much they enjoyed Mack's poetry. Metcalf sent me a poem that Mack had sent to him.

The stone
Of life
Is dropped
Plop...

Into
The well
Of time....
I'm
A ripple
Dimpling
Simply
In
My wide
Decided
Circle
For
The wall
To slide
Limply
Out
Of Mind
Into the troubled
Dregs
Of time
To find
My stone

The next was given to Irina by their secretary who added this note to Irina:

I thought you would like this one. It was written for you (Irina) over 40 years before he met you...

I
want
My Love
To be
Joy
So
Total
Even

Love's
Absence
Cannot
Make
Permanent
Sorrow....

And finally another favorite quote that Mack had told Metcalf "many writers seek to be read between the lines. I want to be read in the lines. To do this, I try to think between words." I was trying to think about the words and the life that generated them.

Mack Thomas has left nothing for posterity. He did not seek glory, fame, or celebrity. Instead he led his own life in his own way. Each time I receive a new email from Irina my heart sinks a little bit. His health slowly deteriorates. He either holds his own or loses some ground.

POSTSCRIPT

I had finished my thesis and been awarded a master's degree in Literature. I began thinking about sharing Mack with a wider audience. I had just visited Mack and Irina in early February. Normally a teacher would not have time to leave his/her classroom in the middle of a semester. However, I had been invited to share my research on a panel at the American Pop Culture Conference just down the road in Albuquerque. My wife and I left the conference for a day and made the drive north. Mack was struggling both physically and mentally during our visit. Later Irina explained that he was having periods of complete clarity followed by periods of forgetfulness. We kept our visit short and left him to nap. I chuckled a bit as we left his room remembering that he always said his favorite position was prone.

As we sat in the living room Irina mentioned that they had found the key to the file cabinet that contained Mack's papers. She had the cabinet brought from El Rito to Santa Fe. She asked if I was interested in looking through the files. Of course I eagerly jumped at the offer. One of the first files I opened was an outline for an episode of the TV series Banacek. For anyone who remembers the show, the outline seemed like a classic episode. A high rise building had been built around a very large safe. Somehow the safe had been stolen. In the final scene Banacek rides in on top of the safe suspended from a crane with the mystery solved. The writing was fast paced and clever.

The rejection letter was also fast paced but not so clever. They loved the script but there were no locations available to film the episode. The producers were going to keep an eye out in case it would ever be possible. The letter ended with please continue to send us scripts.

I also saw a few short stories, what appeared to be a novel or two, private letters, business letters, fragments of poems and prose, and miscellaneous pieces of paper. There was even a postcard delivered to Mack when he was in prison that was signed Bill. The only Bill I was familiar with that Mack knew in 1962 was William Burroughs. I wondered if that postcard was from him. Irina's time was devoted to the 2016 version of Mack living in the next room not the 1960s writer whose works were spread out in front of us on the kitchen table. Again, this would have to wait for another time.

The email from Irina Thomas arrived on February 27, 2016, and simply read "Mack passed away this morning." Of course this was not unexpected but I still needed to stare at the screen for a few minutes for the message to take hold. Mack had been close to death three times in his life, once as an infant, nursed back to health by his sister, as a young man in Germany, and later in the 1980s here in the United States. I remembered that when I started this journey in the back of my mind I thought I was looking for his death certificate. Still I felt a loss. I also felt the pain that his close friends and family must be feeling. Irina had been Mack's lifeline, his constant companion and clearly the love of his life, which also meant he was her life. I'm not certain how she survived the stress.

There were not much in the way of a funeral. Mack was true in death as he was in life, a private person. Eventually Irina was joined by her family and Moises, Mack's friend of 40 years as they quietly spread his ashes beneath an apple tree at his El Rito home. There cannot be a quieter or more beautiful final resting place. It is the place that Mack was happiest. A place that only invited guests would ever find. From beneath that tree you can hear the El Rito River trickle across boulders. You can see the mountains just beyond the small meadow that he and Moises had cleared years before. The clear mountain air allow for the seasonal aroma of apple blossoms to delight the lucky person standing there. Each visitor to the house will pass very near the tree. The location is so much closer to the feelings in *Gumbo* than in *The Total Beast*. Perhaps there Mack has forgotten the ugly five-year chapter of his life in a Texas Prison.

Irina contacted me in May. She was slowly coming to terms with Mack's passing. She was spending some time in Europe with friends and was retracing segments of Mack's life. I received a photo she took of the Beat Hotel in Paris. She sounded a little less weary. She was planning a memorial service for Mack in July and wanted me to save the date. We knew that July 9th we would be in El Rito with Mack's friends to celebrate his life. I knew that would be the final chapter in this book.

And that is how we were once again making the drive to New Mexico from Texas with Mack Thomas on our minds. While we knew more than that first trip, the most important bit of information I learned was that Mack was a master at being a private person and I would never know even a small part of his life. Mack chose his friends carefully and they have special attributes. They are loyal to his wishes which meant they do not tell stories easily about Mack. They guard his privacy almost as much as Mack did himself. They are also intelligent. Intelligent on a wide range of subjects. I was looking forward to meeting them in person to see if Mack's passing had loosened any lips.

We arrived in El Rito several days before the memorial. As always, Irina's hospitality was immense. We were invited to stay in the artist's studio, a short walk across the bridge from the main house. The studio consists of a utility room, a galley style kitchen with lots of windows, a small dining area next to the kitchen, a large bedroom with king size bed and lots of bookcases, and the main showcase, a 25-foot by 20-foot studio lined with windows looking out into the woods. At one end of the studio was a massive table that once belonged in the Governor's Palace. No one seems to know how it came to be in El Rito and no one was surprised or found it unusual. At the other end was a fireplace. Four comfortable chairs were placed at each compass point. Taking up residence in one chair was a very large stuffed bear that had been given to Mack for his 80th birthday. That bear scared the life out of me a couple of times when I entered the room at night.

In the room were Mack's papers. I had several days to comb through the files. Irina was staying in the main house and preparing for the memorial service. She was expecting 30 to 40 guests and preparing food for 100. My wife elected to help with the cooking, leaving me alone with the files.

For weeks, I had been thinking through a strategy for organizing the papers, and decided that the easiest way was to make two piles. One for writings that should be shared and another pile for private material. That worked for a few minutes. I decided to further divide the material into novels, short stories, plays, and scripts. It became obvious there was a lot of material here. I was trying to move quickly yet so many of the stories hooked me and I found myself settling into the chair and reading. The piles were growing on the governor's ten-foot table.

Handling the private letters required a bit of soul searching on my part. I don't think of myself as a professional biographer. I do not trace my craft back to Boswell. I am a learner more comfortable reading the research of others. Here I was reading a letter that I knew Mack may not have shared. There wasn't time to read them all, but a few illuminated some of Mack's writing and I believe are important to share.

Earlier I had formed a hypothesis that sweet *Gumbo* was written prior to Mack entering prison and that the courser *The*

Total Beast was written afterwards. In between would be the events that caused Mack's writing to become darker and more violent. That overly simplistic theory was wrong. *Gumbo* was written while Mack was in prison. In an earlier interview Mack said he wrote *Gumbo* because "it was easy". I found myself holding a letter that Mack had written to his publisher telling the publisher that he could produce a *Gumbo* short story daily. They were very easy to write. He also spoke of his other works that he hoped to have published. He seemed to have preferred those to *Gumbo*. After reading a few, I believe he was right. They are very good.

    A thread ran through many letters: Mack's attempts to be paroled and how he was coping. He mentions that writing was keeping him sane, that he needed to write to mentally escape confinement. Mack went into prison when he was in his late 20s, and if he had served his entire sentence, he would be close to 50 when he was released. Fortunately, he was eligible for parole after four years. Grove Press had written a letter of support citing Mack's considerable talent and predicted a long successful career for Mack as an author. The Texas Board of Pardons and Parole had approved Mack's parole request. Mack had a plan to marry a young lady named Cheryl and move to New York with her and her son. He had a standing job offer from his publisher Grove Press. It would seem his life was about to change for the better. The only thing left was for the governor of Texas, Price Daniels to accept the recommendation of the board.

    Daniels vetoed the request citing his long standing policy of not knowingly approving the parole of people convicted of narcotics violations. This was understandably a harsh turn of events for Mack and his family. This was in October of 1962. A couple of months later his father came to visit him in prison. Mack's father's health was not great at the time. Mack's family believes that the stress of travel and perhaps seeing Mack imprisoned was what led to his dad's sudden passing in December of 1962 just 15 hours after their visit.

Fortunately, Mack was granted a reprieve to attend the funeral. The events in *The Total Beast* basically follow the real life events. He was granted an extension of time but events fell in place that allowed Mack to return to prison at the originally agreed-upon time. In a letter to the board thanking them for the kindness they showed in granting the reprieve, Mack mentioned how difficult it was to be free while knowing he needed to return to prison. That took a moment to sink in. The stress of knowing he had to return to prison was worse than returning to prison. So he went back sooner than the reprieve required.

Eventually Daniels' term as governor ended, the public was embracing a less draconian attitude towards drugs, and Mack was released. Like many, many women in Mack's life, no one knows who Cheryl was and why she was not at the gate to start a life together with Mack.

I placed the file folder of private letters aside and reached back for another file. The short story I pulled out grabbed my attention. I forgot about Mack Thomas Texas inmate and returned to Mack Thomas author. This story was not revealing itself easily. Symbolism was everywhere, meaning was obfuscated, and the story would only become clear with effort on the reader's part. Perhaps this was one of the stories that was rejected for being "ahead of its time" or "not a good fit for our readership"- comments that were consistent in the few rejection letters I read. I tossed it on the stack marked short stories and picked up another. This time what struck me was how Mack signed this typed copy:

Mack Thomas
Box 32
Huntsville, Texas

I knew Mack never voluntarily lived in Huntsville. I reached back in the stack of short stories and flipped to their final pages. Almost every story was signed the same way.

Evidently the bulk of what I had been reading was written while Mack was in prison. I was always puzzled why his literary output decreased so suddenly and his music interest flourished. Now I believe writing brought back unpleasant memories. Playing jazz represented the spontaneity and freedom that had been taken away from him. I suspect that easy theory will ultimately not fit Mack who was never easy.

It was getting late in the day so I decided to walk to the main house. As I left the studio and crossed the small foot bridge the smells were intoxicating. Preparations for the memorial service were in full swing. Lamb chops were being marinated, Mack's favorite meat loaf recipe was in the works (walnuts are the secret ingredient), chickens were being roasted, Irina was overseeing her special "Russian Caviar", bottles of wine were being staged, the house was being transformed into a banquet hall. On the sad side, several expected guests were having problems getting to El Rito.

Jim Metcalf, Mack's closest friend, was stuck in Dallas with his chances of attending slipping away by the second. I had found several typed transcripts of conversations that Mack had recorded with Jim. The subjects were as varied as could be: from concrete subjects like business ventures and housing to philosophical matters that may have been chemically fueled. I was really hoping to show them to Jim and discuss the scenes. That will have to wait for another day as well. Another noticeable cancellation was Don Meredith's widow. Don and Mack were golfing buddies and the couple had gotten together often in Palm Springs and El Rito. I heard she could be outspoken and perhaps I could have picked up an interesting story or two. There were whispers that she may not have liked Mack and the influences Mack had had on her husband.

As we were standing in the middle of a massive amount of pre- party work, Irina announced we were going to Ojo Caliente for a mud bath and dinner. I include this simply as an indicator of Irina's graciousness as a hostess. We were there on a working vacation and to pay our respects to Mack. We were feeling indebted to Irina for her kindness and consideration in allowing us to stay in the studio and to poke through Mack's files. It seemed as if we were stretching the boundaries of being good guests. Our attempts to decline were ignored and soon we were on our way to the resort about thirty minutes away. I doubt any writer has enjoyed the hospitality of the people they are interviewing more than I have enjoyed the hospitality of Mack, Irina, and their friends.

The next day was the memorial service which was starting at noon. At 11:00 A.M. I was still sorting through Mack's files and future projects were becoming clearer. Irina is interested in preserving Mack's work and had been asking for direction. I stepped backed and started counting. There were two full-length novels, three short novels, over two dozen short stories, four plays, several binders of interviews he conducted while researching the connection between drug use and creativity, and a large folder of poems. The rest were musings, legal papers, notes, letters to friends, and odds and ends. In a general sense, I was filling in some gaps while gaps were spreading in other areas. Perhaps some of the guests would be able to offer some help.

As the guests arrived a common theme emerged. Mack had a lot of talented, well-educated friends in a wide range of fields. Most of the crowd met Mack in the previous six to eight years in Santa Fe. There were also friends from El Rito. Mack's niece Diana was there from Dallas with her two children. The food was served and guests pilled plates high with food, poured themselves glasses of wine and moved outside to the tables. Glasses were raised in Mack's honor, toasts said, and the stories flowed.

Mack was a playboy and had many girlfriends through the years. Any mention of Mack and women was met by giggles from the men and women. Repeatedly this was followed by how quickly Mack fell in love with Irina and he became a one-woman man. It was impossible to be at El Rito and not talk about all the work that Mack had done on the home. Moises was a wealth of information with the history of the house.

El Rito's remoteness was what attracted Mack to the area. He could live without much constraints. In the time that I spent in the area I never saw the police. People need to be self-reliant. Moises added to the story regarding a series of buildings that had been set on fire around the area. Perhaps it was random, perhaps the newer settlers to the area were targeted. Either way Mack was concerned about his property. Moises grew up in the area and was well known to everyone. He helped Mack keep vigilance day and night until the danger had passed. Moises feels that helped cement their relationship.

Speaking about the craftsmanship of the home Moises recalled building the solarium. Mack came in one day to check on the progress and found a wall 1/16" off. That was deemed unacceptable and they tore the wall down and rebuilt it from the floor up. As we looked around the grounds Moises explained the origins of the materials, how things were built, and how much Mack enjoyed the processes from design to completion.

The sun was beginning to become unbearable and the guests began migrating to the main house. Glasses were raised, the food was praised and some of the same stories were repeated. Interestingly the stories of Mack's childhood were basically retelling of the stories from Gumbo, this time with the actual names. Small details were being revealed. Pud, the pseudonym used for Mack's younger brother Roy, was his actual nickname which was earned by his love of banana pudding. Mack had been very sick with cholera as an infant and his sister, no older than seven at the time had indeed fed him water with an eye dropper and nursed him back to health. It seems that most of Mack's friend had read Gumbo, less had read The Total Beast. So it wasn't a surprise that most of the stories seemed to be ripped from those pages. People assumed

I knew more than I did. I could provide some background but in the end we realized Mack had been private.

Howard Ruben, Mack's Hollywood agent arrived after the memorial was in full swing. Howard lives just up the road from Mack's place. Decades earlier Howard had pursued Mack as a client. Howard had visited El Rito to help convince Mack he needed an agent and that agent should be Howard. As Mack was showing him the area Howard remarked that he would like to own property in the area. Eventually a piece of property became available and Howard took his place in a long line of successful people from all over the world who make the mountains north of Santa Fe home.

I had been wanting to ask Howard about The Total Beast and the movie deal that had fallen through. As I mentioned earlier when Peppard's name came up Mack called Peppard an "asshole". The assumption had been that Mack and Peppard did not get along and that friction caused the deal to fall through. Howard told a different version.

Howard had introduced Mack to Peppard who was also his client. Being a good agent he was looking to package the movie and include his clients. Earlier in 1974 Howard had Mack brought in to help rewrite the script for Newman's Law which starred Peppard. During this period Peppard was a hot actor and would bring some star power to the project. Mack had observed that Peppard was perhaps too old to properly portray Mack's character in the movie. Both men were born in 1928 which made Peppard more than ten years older than Mack was while in prison. But the two of them hit it off and were getting along very well, perhaps too well. Mack and Peppard decided to package the movie themselves and bypassed Howard.

Mack and Peppard went directly to a producer and in Howard's telling made it seem as if they were doing the producer a favor in offering the movie to him. Their collective egos did not allow themselves to take the humbler approach that Ruben felt was necessary to have a movie made at the time. It is difficult to dispute Howard's assessment because the movie was never made. With the current popularity of Orange is the New Black perhaps the time is right for a period prison movie.

Mack's niece Diana, she is the daughter of Roy Thomas, helped fill in some of the details and Mack's involvement with Thomas Plastics. Roy was working in the plastics industry when he found himself at the age of fifty unemployed, a victim of a misunderstanding with the owner of the company he was working for. The owner believed, erroneously, that Roy was lining things up to start his own business. Left without many options Roy elected to start a business. He had the expertise and contacts at a couple potential customers. What he lacked was the capital. Mack had equity in his El Rito home and purchased an interest in the company. This is different than earlier versions I heard which had Mack using book royalties as collateral.

Guests slowly trickled in and out until finally Irina was able to take a deep breath and sit down. I congratulated her on a wonderful memorial service. We drained the last of a bottle of wine and made plans to look over Mack's materials in the morning.

When Irina arrived the next morning I had neatly arranged stacks for her to look at. The smallest pile were personal letters pertaining to his time in prison and the attempts for parole, business letters, a couple rejection letters, and similar. The unpublished material was a far bigger pile. Mack completed a couple full length novels that he may never have submitted to publishers, a couple short novels, a screen play, dozens of short stories, and a thick pile of poems. "Where to start" was Irina's question.

I am confident that some more of Mack's work will be available soon. Irina is planning on pairing Mack's poetry with her artwork. Those that know them both all agree this will be a beautiful collaboration. Additional plans are to review the novels for publication. The short stories will be edited and curated and the collection made available either electronically or in print.

As a biography this effort leaves many more questions than answers. As a memoir it is fairly complete. Each time I put my pen down and think I am finished another lead pops up, someone offers a story. I decided to pause here not because the rest of Mack's story is uninteresting, I am certain it is not. I am pausing here to allow Mack his peace. To offer some literary room for his stories to be published that have been unknown to most everyone. The only person who could have made Mack famous was Mack. He chose to live comfortably away from any publicity in El Rito. His friends know him as a genius. He was loved and admired by people he loved and admired. Perhaps that is the best lesson.

REFERENCES

Burroughs, William S., and Oliver Harris. Junky. New York: Penguin, 2003. Print.

Burroughs, William S. Queer. New York, NY: Penguin, 1987. Print.

Carmona, Christopher, Rob Johnson, and Chuck Taylor. The Beatest State in the Union: An Anthology of Beat Texas Writings. N.d. MS. N.p.

Charters, Ann. The Portable Beat Reader. New York, NY: Penguin, 1992. Print.

Davis, Steven L. Texas Literary Outlaws: Six Writers in the Sixties and beyond. Fort Worth, TX: TCU, 2004. Print.

Johnson, Rob. The Lost Years of William S. Burroughs: Beats in South Texas. College Station: Texas A & M UP, 2006. Print.

Kerouac, Jack. On the Road. New York: Penguin, 1976. Print.

Miles, Barry. The Beat Hotel: Ginsberg, Burroughs, and Corso in Paris, 1958-1963. New York: Grove, 2000. Print.

Miles, Barry. Call Me Burroughs: A Life. N.p.: n.p., n.d. Print.

Morgan, Ted. Literary Outlaw: The Life and times of William S. Burroughs. New York: W.W. Norton, 2012. Print.

Thomas, Mack. Gumbo. New York: Grove, 1965. Print.

Thomas, Mack. The Total Beast; a Novel. New York: Simon and Schuster, 1970. Print.

Watson, Steven. The Birth of the Beat Generation: Visionaries, Rebels, and Hipsters, 1944-1960. New York: Pantheon, 1995. Print.

ABOUT THE AUTHOR

Jim Welton is a lifelong student who lefty snowy Chicago for the sunshine of Texas. His career matches his wide range of interests from business, where he rose to be the vice president of sales, to his current calling as a high school English educator. When not reading, writing, and researching Welton can be found on the golf course and hiking and backpacking our National Parks.

www.ingramcontent.com/pod-product-compliance
Lightning Source LLC
Chambersburg PA
CBHW032020040426
42448CB00006B/678